"Mary DeMuth is a real mom dealing with the real issues moms face. If you ever wonder if God really cares about PMS, sticky kitchen floors, and children who ask incessant questions, then this book is for you! In her honest, mom-next-door way, Mary shares with you God's perspective and encouragement you are longing to hear."

—Jill Savage,
founder and executive
director of Hearts at Home

"Mary DeMuth may be an ordinary mom, but she writes about mothering with extraordinary grace and wit. This is a book for every mother who yearns to hear the footfalls of Jesus in her home and to feel His tender touch in her soul."

—Jan Winebrenner,
author of *Intimate Faith*

"What a tall mocha is to coffee lovers, Mary DeMuth is to devotional writing. Refreshing, habit-forming, and even better when shared with a friend."

—Sandra Glahn, ThM,
bestselling author

ORDINARY
MOM
EXTRAORDINARY
GOD

MARY E.
DeMUTH

HARVEST HOUSE PUBLISHERS

EUGENE, OREGON

Published in association with the literary agency of Alive Communications, Inc., 7680 Goddard Street, Suite 200, Colorado Springs, CO 80920

Cover by Terry Dugan Design, Minneapolis, Minnesota

ORDINARY MOM, EXTRAORDINARY GOD
Copyright © 2005 by Mary E. DeMuth
Published by Harvest House Publishers
Eugene, Oregon 97402
www.harvesthousepublishers.com

Library of Congress Cataloging-in-Publication Data
DeMuth, Mary E., 1967-
  Ordinary mom, extraordinary God / Mary E. DeMuth.
    p. cm.
  Includes bibliographical references.
  ISBN-13: 978-0-7369-1500-7
  ISBN-10: 0-7369-1500-1
  1. Mothers—Religious life. I. Title.
BV4529.18.D46 2005
242'.6431—dc22
                                                          2004015789

Printed in the United States of America

07   08   09   10   11   12   / VP-CF /   10   9   8   7   6   5   4   3

To Patrick, whose life teaches me that God is love.
To Sophie, Aidan, and Julia, who surprise
me daily with snapshots of his joy.

To Jesus, who dares to hold my hand when I walk,
picks me up when I fall, and sets my feet upon a rock.

CONTENTS

HE'S THE
EXTRAORDINARY ONE

I'M AN ORDINARY MOM just like you. In the mundane of life, in line at the grocery store, on soccer sidelines, I perform the ordinary tasks of motherhood. But this is no ordinary task, raising children. It takes perseverance, grit, and a day-by-day, minute-by-minute encounter with our extraordinary God.

I write this book from my own mothering weaknesses. I fail often. Yet in that failure, our extraordinary God has picked me up, dusted me off, and whispered words of encouragement to my tired heart.

These whispered words are now written for you in the pages of this book. *Ordinary Mom, Extraordinary God* represents my parenting journey from Christmas Eve 1992, the day Sophie was born, to the present—where Sophie is a tenderhearted "tween" at eleven, Aidan is a budding Lego architect at eight, and Julia is a silly-hearted kindergartener who has broken her arms three times. Their lives, intertwined with mine, have been the proving ground for God's extraordinary strength.

I pray this book would be an encouragement to you—that you'd hear the whisper of your Savior as you change diapers, that you'd sense his pleasure as you swing with your children, toes kissing the sky, and that you'd delight in his extraordinary strength when yours wanes.

1

AND A HAPPY NEW EAR

*J*ULIA, MY YOUNGEST, and Aidan, our middle child, had a fight. She was singing a rather raucous rendition of "We Wish You a Merry Christmas." Aidan, unaware of the flurry that would soon befall him, intertwined his boy choir voice with hers and finished "and a happy New Year."

Julia cocked her head, her blonde hair jutting to one side. "Aidan, you are singing that wrong."

"No, I'm not, Julia."

"Yes, you are."

"No, I'm not," he seconded, this time in a higher pitch—like a clearly rendered high C.

"Yes, you are," she replied plainly. "It's supposed to be 'and a Happy New *Ear*.' You are wrong."

At this point I turned from the spectacle and laughed. When I regained my momlike composure, as any good authority figure should, I told Julia, "Actually, Julia, Aidan *is* right. It is Happy New *Year*, not *Ear*."

"No, it's not, Mommy. You are wrong."

Perhaps I am. We all need Merry Christmases. And many of us need Happy New Ears. I realized that truth when I read about a man and his family during a particular boom to a small Washington state village in the late 1800s. Gold-hungry folks crowded into that tiny community, creating great amounts of construction, mayhem, laughter, vitality, and even a printing press.

When the Canadian government required these "settlers" to get a license in Canada to hunt the elusive metal, everyone except the initial Washington settlers fled, leaving behind shells of homes, useless acres full of mud, and fallen trees.

When the last schooner pulled away, the family's patriarch looked up to the sky because he heard something. It was the lilting song of the ducks. He had forgotten them. All the noise had blotted their song from him during the summertime boom. For a day he simply sat and listened to the ducks.

I need to listen to the ducks. I need to listen more to everything—the "Mommy pleases," the nuances of sadness in my preteen daughter, the friendly voice of my son in his simple joy over creating a model, the cat's purr, a friend's tired voice, my husband's perplexing over theological questions. These nuances need to be mined rather than ignored.

But to listen well we have to make a choice. To have a new ear, we have to blot out other distractions that pepper us all day long. The seemingly important things—the things that assail from left and right, from above and beneath—are like tiny insidious monsters, pulling us in directions we never intended to go. They have loud voices, disguised in ringing telephones, ding-donging doorbells, blaring televisions, static-loving radios.

There are days I just want to throw my tired hands to the sky and shout, "Enough!" in some sort of poetic declaration to the noise gods that I will not listen. It's not really their fault. I have to learn to turn things off, to not clutter my life with so much noise. I can't hear the important things if the unimportant clamor minute by minute for my attention. "This is what the Sovereign LORD, the Holy One of Israel, says: 'In repentance and rest is your salvation, and quietness and trust is your strength, but you would have none of it'" (Isaiah 30:15).

If I disdain repentance, rest, quietness, and trust, I will not hear what God wants me to hear. I will be tossed here and there by noise, neglecting the cries of my children or stifling the cry of my heart to be quiet before Jesus.

Many times the noise I refuse to quiet is my own, coming from deep inside me. Its voice utters words like "should," "you'd better," or "so you can cross that off your list." When I listen to these voices, I am more apt to snap at my children's innocent needs or miss a friend's nonverbal plea for a listening ear.

The only remedy for a loud life and an ear bent away from listening to the important is to cry out to God. "Then they cried out to the LORD in their trouble, and he brought them out of their distress. He stilled the storm to a whisper; the waves of the sea were hushed. They were glad when it grew calm, and he guided them to their desired haven" (Psalm 107:28-30).

Only the Lord who stills the seas can bend my ear toward him and others. For him to perform that auditory surgery, I need to cry out to him. With that in mind, I will sing *and a Happy New Ear* with glee.

Dear Jesus, give me new ears. Mine are full of noise right now, and I can't seem to have any auditory peace. Help me to welcome stillness. Lead me, as the psalmist declared, beside quiet waters. Keep me attuned to the cries of this world—the deeper needs that go unmet because everyone is busy listening to other noise. I want to be your ears today—to my children, my spouse, and your world.

2

MOMMY, I'D
BE GLADITUDE

NE DAY, WHEN I ASKED my daughter Julia to clean her room, I expected a high-pitched whine or a stomping of little feet. Instead she said, "Mommy, I'd be gladitude."

A wordsmith, I knew her morphing of "glad to" and "attitude" was improper, but the truth of her words resonated with me. How much more delightful it was to watch Julia clean her room with "gladitude" than with a scowl. I wondered how much God must delight when we perform our motherly duties in a like manner, thanking him along the way. This is what I call GQ—our Gladitude Quotient.

My friend Hud specializes in GQs. He loves saying, "There is no neutral space between ingratitude and gratitude." His point is that we are either grateful or not, and that most Christians settle for wallowing in a complaint-based life.

If complaining marks our motherhood, we can ignore the deeper truths God wants to teach us, missing those fleeting growth opportunities God places in our path. Often, his growth plan includes mother-in-law tension, rebellious children, tired husbands, dirty dishes, snippy checkout ladies, or muddy shoes on new carpet. It's in those moments our GQ is tested.

More than his presence in the difficulties, what we really desire is a stress-free life—full of supportive mother-in-laws, obedient children, helpful husbands, clean dishes, smiling checkout ladies, and muddy shoes outside on the doorstep. When God throws mountain-sized wrenches in our hope for a stress-free life, we tend to pout instead of praise.

The Message renders Psalm 116:5-8 this way: "God is gracious—it is he who makes things right, our most compassionate God. God takes the side of the helpless; when I was at the end of my rope, he saved me. I said to myself, 'Relax and rest. God has showered you with blessings. Soul, you've been rescued from death; Eye, you've been rescued from tears; and you, Foot, were kept from stumbling.'"

The key to the psalmist's ability to live a thankful life was his ability to stop, rest, and consider what God had done for him. As harried mothers with rolling hills of laundry, crying children, and sticky floors, we need to endeavor to become motherly psalmists who say, "Return to your rest, O my soul, for the LORD has dealt bountifully with you" (Psalm 116:7 NASB).

Even with laundry piled to the windows, we can be grateful that the God who clothes the lilies has graciously chosen to clothe us. Even amid the crying mayhem, we can remember God has blessed our children with healthy lungs. Even when our jogging shoes stick to the kitchen floor, we can thank him for the floors and the Kool-Aid that stains them. My theologian son, Aidan, understands the importance of thankfulness. One day he prayed, "God is great. God is good. Let us thank him for our *mood*."

I wish I could pray that prayer with confidence—that I possessed such a thankful mood I could praise God for it. God *is* great. God *is* good. He will gladly transform my mood.

After Jacob wrestled with God in the town of Bethel, he exclaimed, "Surely the LORD is in this place, and I was not aware of it" (Genesis 28:16). Could it be that the Lord is in your home and you are not aware of his footfalls? That you have forgotten to thank him for his tangible presence even when your child swallows a penny? That you've forgotten the importance of "gladitude"?

L.B. Cowman in the landmark devotional *Streams in the Desert* said, "It is easier to sing your worries away than to reason them away."[1] Toys break. Tempers flare. Milk spills. Life is full of harmony-busters. May we remember that elusive GQ as we sing praises to the God who gave us the amazing privilege of motherhood.

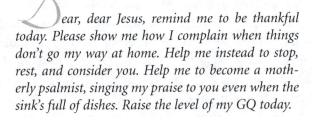

Dear, dear Jesus, remind me to be thankful today. Please show me how I complain when things don't go my way at home. Help me instead to stop, rest, and consider you. Help me to become a motherly psalmist, singing my praise to you even when the sink's full of dishes. Raise the level of my GQ today.

3

THE NERVOUS
PIE EATER

WHEN AIDAN WAS TWO, he was a biter. One day he bit his five-year-old sister Sophie, who after crying told me, "Maybe Aidan was nervous and thought I was pie."

When we attended the orientation for our mission's agency, the HR (human resources) guy told us one of the striking attributes of marriages that thrived was this: The spouses assumed positive intent. In other words, instead of jumping to wrong conclusions when a spouse did something catty, the offended spouse was able to assume the best instead of the worst. It's an interesting measuring gauge for marriage. When our spouses wrong us, do we automatically assume they had negative intent? A sign of a healthy marriage is giving each other the blessed benefit of the doubt.

Once Patrick was late coming home and I was not assuming positive intent. I invented all sorts of reasons for his tardiness in my head—he was working late again even though he knew I hated that; he was getting his truck serviced without first telling me; he was fishing with a friend from work. When he came in an hour later, I was ready to let him have it. Thankfully, I kept quiet for a blessed nanosecond. From behind his back he presented a bouquet of red roses. Behind him stood our babysitter. That evening, the husband I assumed was a rapscallion swept me off my feet and took me on a romantic date!

Assuming positive intent spills over into effective parenting. How often have I assumed negative intent with my children? How quick am I to jump to the worst conclusion when kids come in crying after bicycle riding.

"Who pushed Julia off her bike? Did you, Aidan?"

"No, Mommy. I didn't. She fell."

The Message renders 1 Corinthians 13:7 this way: "[Love] puts up with anything, trusts God always, *always looks for the best*, never looks back, but keeps going to the end" (emphasis mine). In my zeal to be a parent with children who obey at my first insistence, I have forgotten the aspect of love that looks for the best in my children. Instead of viewing them as allies in our family's corporate struggle against sin and the enemy of our souls, I see them as combatants—and I often fail to assume positive intent.

Last week Julia came in crying, holding her face. "Aidan tried to kill me," she said.

"Is that true?" I asked, narrowing my eyes. I assumed it was.

"No, Mommy," Aidan said. "She just wouldn't get out of the way when I was throwing the football."

Upon further investigation, I realized both were at fault, but I riled Aidan by assuming his intent was to "kill." Instead, I wished I would have held them on my lap and listened, letting their sordid tales spill from their mouths without inflaming passions.

Assuming negative intent, whether with our children or spouse, has a lot to do with judging hastily. Jesus said, "For in the same way you judge others, you will be judged, and with the measure you use, it will be measured to you" (Matthew 7:2). Jumping to quick judgment is the antithesis to grace and invites a similar judgment in return.

Our friend Wade infuses his parenting with grace. When one of his children disobeys, he asks them their side of the story before rendering judgment. Sometimes he says, "Yeah, well, that's pretty bad. I will have to punish you. It's what you deserve." Other times he surprises the offending child by saying, "That was bad, but I am not going to punish you." He then explains about God's mercy, that because of Jesus we receive mercy and don't have to live eternally separated from God. On rare occasions, Wade says, "Yes, what you did was wrong. Let's go have ice cream." Over a cone he explains the outrageous grace of God—that not only does he give us mercy and save us from hell, but he also gives us abundant life, even when we don't deserve it.

Wade assumes positive intent and then takes parenting a step further by revealing the nature of God's judgment, mercy, and grace.

After Aidan's teeth permeated Sophie's skin, she assumed positive intent by equating her skin with pie. Hers was an act of grace, of assuming positive intent.

Dear Jesus, I want to assume positive intent in my marriage. Instruct me on how I can perform this grace-filled act with my children. Help me not to rush to judgment. Thank you for showing me your mercy and grace so I can exemplify your heart toward them.

4

THE PRUNING HAND
OF GOD

Clee

ADMIRE GARDENERS LIKE my neighbors Jimmy and
Tessie, who have gumdrop-pruned shrubbery. I, however, have a
wild yard splayed with a riot of flowers. My theory is that I was
born to live in England, in an ancient stone cottage with an
abundance of wild roses clinging to walls and arbors.

My children like to give our climbing roses to their teachers.
This kind act both delights and vexes me—*delights* because I
want my roses to cheer up teachers, and *vexes* because the roses
are usually plucked from the wrong part of the rosebush, leaving
them gangly. Toward the lower half of my climbers, there's a
child-shaped void where only foliage exists—where the roses
have been plucked by my flower-giving children.

Live as a mother *and* a gardener for any length of time, and
you will encounter the innocent pruning hands of little ones.
Thankfully, my resilient roses have flourished, birthing new
roses for new teachers. Eventually the child-shaped void flour-
ishes.

Pruning reminds me of something Jesus said. "If you, then,
though you are evil, know how to give good gifts to your children, how much more will your Father in heaven give good gifts

to those who ask him!" (Matthew 7:11). If children, unlikely horticulturists that they are, haphazardly prune my roses, how much more can the Holy Gardener prune my life?

To prune is to cut and reshape a plant in order to remove anything preventing or diminishing vitality. Drive the dusty foothills of Provence, France, and you will see field upon field of grapevines twisted around stakes. There's nothing spectacular about them, especially in winter when they look like forgotten sticks. A well-pruned vineyard looks stark. Dead. But only the pruned vineyard produces fruit.

Likewise, my motherhood is often the tool God uses to prune me in order to produce healthy fruit. Before children, the garden of my spiritual life seemed productive, with neat rows and happy plants. Children upset my tried-and-true "quiet time." Their late-night feedings wore my patience thin. Their inherent neediness exposed my selfish heart. My spiritual garden had grown out of control. Children revealed to me my need for the Gardener, for his gentle pruning hand.

He is the One who said, "I am the true vine, and my Father is the gardener. He cuts off every branch in me that bears no fruit, while every branch that does bear fruit he prunes so that it will be even more fruitful" (John 15:1-2). He desires mothers to bear much fruit, that our character would become more like his— gentle, humble, and grateful. He wants to reap fruit from the vines of our lives, fruit that he produces, fruit that brings him glory, fruit that beckons a dying world to himself. "The fruit of the Spirit is love, joy, peace, patience, kindness, goodness, faithfulness, gentleness and self-control. Against such things there is no law" (Galatians 5:22-23).

When life is crazy and children are screaming, remember that the Gardener is using these very circumstances to prune your self-sufficiency. Remember the hopeful truth that the Vinedresser is never closer to the branches than when he is pruning them. He is nearest you when he prunes, and his pruning will make you a better worshiper, wife, and mother.

Don't shrink back from his pruning. Don't think he's come to destroy you. His pruning, when viewed through the lenses of eternity and the kingdom of God, makes for fruit that lasts. "You did not choose me, but I chose you and appointed you to go and bear fruit—fruit that will last" (John 15:16).

The fruit he produces through his nearness is something we can offer him when we get to heaven. Like my daughter Julia who said, "When I get to heaven, I want to give God a big bouquet of flowers," we can offer him our changed, pure heart.

Dear Lord, show me the places in my life that are unruly, that need your tender pruning. Thank you for using my children as tools to prune my character. Teach me to welcome your gardening hand. Help me to want to be fruitful and to understand that before I can bloom, you have to cut.

5

WHICH SISTER
ARE YOU?

*J*ULIA ASKED ME ONE DAY, out of the clear blue Texas sky, "Do you want me to be Cinderella or wicked?"

"Why, Cinderella, of course."

She smiled. Mirrored in her deep brown eyes, I could almost see a twirling Cinderella donning her godmother-spun dress, dancing on slippers of glass.

I want to be Cinderella too. I want to be kind, grateful, self-less, and hardworking. Unfortunately, while cleaning the house in my not-so-glass slippers, bits and pieces of wicked stepsisters push their way into my day. On some particularly PMS-infused days, I morph from happy ash-cleaning Cinderella to pouting self-absorbed stepsister as fast as you can say "hormones."

Do you want to be Cinderella or wicked? Here are some questions to ask yourself:

Do I envy what others have? The wicked stepsisters envied Cinderella's beauty and grace. Do I have a similar bent toward someone? Do I disdain another woman who seems more together than I am? Do I begrudge someone else's success? Her marriage? Her children? Her abilities? Do I spend a lot of thought time thinking how I wish my life were different? Do I use the words "if only" a lot? If only I'd lose weight like her. If only I'd be more holy and have one hour on my knees every day the way she does. If only my husband would instigate family devotions. Consider how The Message renders Galatians 5:26: "That means we will not compare ourselves with each other as if one of us were better and another worse. We have far more interesting things to do with our lives. Each of us is an original."

Do I expect others to do everything for me? The stepsisters were lazy, insisting that Cinderella feed and clothe them. Moms who instill a work ethic in children require them to do chores. In this case, it *is* healthy to have children do things for you—and learn the importance of work ethic. But, what about your *heart?* Do you expect your friends to fill you up? Do you expect your children to fill a God-sized hole in your heart? Do you expect your husband to anticipate your every desire? The only One who can truly fill our hearts is God. If we constantly look to others to fill our hearts, we will become bitter and self-absorbed. Our expectations of others lessen when we make it a habit to pour all our needs at the feet of the Lord. He is the One who promises to "refresh the weary and satisfy the faint" (Jeremiah 31:25).

Am I mean? The stepsisters were downright cruel—tearing at Cinderella's gown, jamming their cloddy feet into her delicate slipper. As a mom, am I mean? Do I treat strangers better than I treat my husband and children? Would I be horrified if the movie of my life were played on a hidden camera reality show? Do my words belittle, degrade, harm, or nag? How would I feel if someone said my words to me? Am I "quick to listen, slow to speak and slow to become angry?" (James 1:19).

Do I pigeonhole? The stepsisters saw Cinderella just one way—as a servant to be treated with contempt. The reality was that she was a princess in distressing disguise. Do I see my children in only one light? Do I expect them to only act a certain way? Have I stifled creativity on the altar of my own desires for my children? Often we misread Proverbs 22:6: "Train a child in the way he should go, and when he is old he will not turn from it." The verse does not read, "Train a child in the way you'd like him to go."

Am I conceited? The stepsisters actually thought they had a chance in wooing the prince! They spent most of their days primping and preening. Am I spending a lot of time thinking about how I appear to others? Not just in the way I dress, but in the way others perceive me? Pride can be defined as preoccupation with self. Whether we lament our looks or parade ourselves in front of others to be noticed, we are prideful. The apostle Paul encourages us to think differently about ourselves: "For by the grace given me I say to everyone of you: Do not think of yourself more highly than you ought, but rather think of yourself with sober judgment, in accordance to the measure of faith God has given you" (Romans 12:3).

Julia's question still rolls around in my mind: *Would you like me to be Cinderella or wicked?* Oh, to be content with cleaning ashes and singing with the birds, with promoting others and having a heart bent toward God, with being quick to listen and giving my children the freedom to be themselves, with having a divine preoccupation instead of a selfish one.

Dear Jesus, how I long to be more like patient, sweet Cinderella. Show me the places in my heart where I resemble the wicked stepsisters. Help me to love the people you place in my life with an authentic, deep-rooted love. Help me to run to you for everything, especially when a wicked stepsister threatens to take over my home.

6

CRYING FOR GOD

*T*HERE ARE TIMES MY PMS HEART could cry like a baby with a turbo diaper rash. There are other times I tell my husband, "Honey, I just need to cry," but the tears stubbornly refuse to cooperate, like a three-year-old boy bent on wearing diapers until kindergarten. As women and mothers, our lives boil over. Sometimes we pour the boiling water back into our pressure cooker and hope for no explosions; other times we spew our frustrations on our unsuspecting children.

But God offers us a third way, a way of escape. He longs to bear our burdens. Listen to him beckon. "Come to me, all you who are weary and burdened, and I will give you rest. Take my yoke upon you and learn from me, for I am gentle and humble in heart, and you will find rest for your souls. For my yoke is easy and my burden is light" (Matthew 11:28-30).

We need to cry to him first. Because he walked the path we walk, he can come alongside us with empathy, understanding, and strength. The author of Hebrews assures, "We do not have a high priest who is unable to sympathize with our weaknesses, but we have one who has been tempted in every way, just as we are—yet without sin. Let us then approach the throne of grace with confidence, so that we may receive mercy and find grace to help us in our time of need" (Hebrews 4:15-16).

Imagine that! Jesus was tempted to scream at his disciples just as we are tempted to scream at our offspring. He was tempted to throw in the linen wrapping just as we are tempted to throw in the kitchen towel. He was exasperated. He felt alone. His glory was unseen. He was unappreciated. He was misunderstood. His own family thought he was crazy. He endured all that, so he will help us endure. He cried tears intermingled with his own blood; he does not despise our tears of salt water.

I like the way the New International Version renders Psalm 118:5: "In my anguish, I cried to the LORD, and he answered by setting me free." The great paradox of life is that grief, when it holds the hand of God, brings joy—that tears, when they wet the throne of God, bring freedom.

Overwhelmed by a messy house, a hurried life, and a fear that I was failing at motherhood, I cried out to God:

My tears are held back in stoic mystery
Capricious, as if the tears know my need
For purging and cleansing
Yet refuse to usher forth

Cry, O soul, cry for God
In that dry and weary place called ordinary
Where no myrrh scents my ambitions
Where no mirth echoes my barren heart
Where few understand deepened grief

Cry, O soul, cry for God
In that hiding place my cry can't escape
When only wind sees my penitence
Where pottery shards of my making crumble still further
Where the house seems swept yet suffers cobwebs

Cry, O soul, cry for God
Cry deep despite harried triviality

Cry deep despite crushing failure
Cry deep despite narrowed eyes bent on destruction

For the dawn will come again
Dewy and sweet
When soul can dance on shattered glass
And suffer no injury

Rejoice again
For tears, once kept hidden
Will yet again emit miracles
Transforming rage to hope
Intermingling loss to life

Cry, O soul, cry for God
His sacred cistern counts each tear
One by one
He tilts it, wetting my upturned head
Washing my countenance with grief
Revealing the blessed paradox
That joy is birthed in tears

Through that catharsis, through reaching for God, who seemed far, I was set free from the darkness of my circumstance. There is no crazy-busy day that God cannot shoulder. There is no dallying in the ordinariness of dishes, diapers, and doughnuts that God cannot redeem. There is no loss of temper that God cannot forgive. Cry to him. Cry *out* to him. He is a mother's burden-bearer.

Jesus, I am overwhelmed by the task of mommy-hood sometimes. I need your help today. Would you take my tears, my frustrations, my failures and hold them near your heart? Will you bring me rest when my life whirrs like the spin cycle? Will you show me it's okay to stop and cry out to you? In my anguish, I do cry out to you. Please answer by setting me free—free to love my family, free to engage fully in the moment, free to set the unimportant aside. I need you.

7

THE DESERT

URING A PARTICULARLY LONELY and dry time in my walk with Jesus, my friend Sue told me, "It looks like God is bringing you through the desert. You won't be there forever, but he has you there now and he will bring you through."

The night before I had read, "The people who survived the sword will find favor in the desert. I will come to give rest to Israel" (Jeremiah 31:2).

After the desert verse and Sue's conversation, I remember thinking, *The desert? Who wants to walk through a desert? There's nothing in a desert. Why would God want me to be here? I'd settle for an oasis.*

Still, I remembered that my greatest growth had come when I held onto Jesus in the dusty desert: during my first pregnancy when I heard the doctor say the word "ectopic"; during lonely nights when my husband was overworked; during the exasperating sameness of diapers and dirty toilets. These were the times God grew me up. I've learned a lot about deserts since then and, knowing the tangles of this life, will learn further still.

The enemy has plans to destroy us when we walk through the desert. I am someone who's *lived through* everything the enemy of my life (Satan) has done to me. He's hurtled all sorts of things my way—sexual abuse, death of a parent, emotional absence of a parent, loneliness, thoughts of suicide. In all that I remember Joseph, who had horrible things happen to him at the hands of his enemies (who happened to be his brothers). What did Joseph say to his brothers after he had become a powerful deliverer from famine in Egypt? "As for you, you meant evil against me, but *God meant it for good* in order to bring about this present result, to preserve many people alive" (Genesis 50:20 NASB, emphasis mine). Joseph recognized the hand of God even in his trials.

Not only will God bring me through the arid land, but he also promises he will supply help in the desert. The desert symbolizes a stripping away of everything in my life that I unwittingly think is concrete. And when I am there, I am more apt to cry than to cry out to the Father. Somehow I want him to change me so I can better cope with motherhood. So I can be strong and face my tasks with grace. So I can be some sort of example to other parents.

As I sit thirsty in the desert, the help he brings is his sufficiency, not mine. He doesn't make me able; he is able. He doesn't craft a perfect clay pot out of my life; he fills the imperfect one with his perfection. Thank goodness my clay pot is cracked, for it is through many imperfections that his glory shines. Paul said, "We have this treasure in earthen vessels, that the surpassing greatness of the power may be of God and not from ourselves" (2 Corinthians 4:7 NASB). God doesn't change my ability to cope with the task of motherhood necessarily; he replaces my heart with his parental heart.

The desert is a dry place, where my thirst is keen. The essentials of life boil down to this statement: I am thirsty and I need a drink. Nothing makes me more aware of the complicated life I lead than when I find myself in the desert. There, ankles dusted, I see only one essential need—water. And when I pare away my mountains of problems, I understand that all I need is a drink of water—a cool drink from the River of Life, Jesus himself.

The woman at the well wanted to know where she could get her hands on some of that never-thirst-again living water. Jesus told her "the water that I will give [you] shall become in [you] a well of water springing up to eternal life" (John 4:14 NASB).

If you are in the desert, thank the Lord. Now you'll see clearly that all you need is his living water. And when you drink deeply of it, you will never have thirst again—the thirst for recognition, the thirst for power, the thirst for youth, the thirst for beauty, the thirst for motherly perfection, the thirst for thrills, the thirst for comfort. Jesus will fill you completely and everything else will pale in comparison. You can only know true joy when you get to the end of yourself and jump headlong into the River of Living Water.

Jesus, I don't like deserts. Would you teach me how to love you in the midst of my dryness? Would you surprise me today with a deep drink of that Living Water you promise? Teach me to thirst only for you. Help me to let your magnificence shine through my cracked-pot life.

8

BECOME AS
A CHILD

N AN UNGUARDED MOMENT, one of life's pure relaxed snapshots, my son asked me, "Can God feel the wind?"

I stopped when he said it—stopped everything I was doing. I realized afresh that parenting was not so much me imparting deep spiritual truth into the hearts of my children, but quite the opposite: My children are God's way of growing me up, of teaching me more about him.

Jesus said, "I tell you the truth, unless you change and become like little children, you will never enter the kingdom of heaven. Therefore, whoever humbles himself like this child is the greatest in the kingdom of heaven. And whoever welcomes a little child like this in my name welcomes me" (Matthew 18:3-5).

Could it be that God gives us children to lead us to him? Could it be that parenting is more learning than teaching? Could it be that what Jesus really wants from us is not capability, but humility enough to learn from the mouths of babes?

Today as you face the whirlwind of life, get on your knees—not necessarily to pray (we can pray when we drive the minivan to the store, for that matter), but to see what life looks like from our children's perspective. With new eyes, wonder at the world

God created. Look up. That's the posture the Lord wants us to have. He wants to be the lifter of our heads. He longs for us to simply look up for his help.

Remember the movie *Big* where Tom Hank's character is a child in an adult's body? How did he interact with the world? Cynically? No, he had a wide-eyed jubilance about life—he played, he jumped on the bed, he smiled. Perhaps the Lord gives us children so we can remember what we once were—carefree and happy to be content with one day.

Dr. Dan Allender, who wrote the book *How Children Raise Parents,* asserts, "Thank God for your children because they are the ones who grow you up into spiritual maturity. Far more than being concerned about how to correct, or convert, or counsel your children, thank God for what your children are teaching you."[2]

It's a topsy-turvy notion that children lead us into maturity, but isn't the kingdom of heaven like that? The poor own it. The humble understand it. The proud disdain it. The capable elude it.

I learn more about the gentleness of Jesus when I dare to apologize to my children. Escalated talk becomes kind embrace—and somehow in the midst of that, I experience the paradoxical kingdom.

I learn more about the wonder of Jesus when I watch the stars with Aidan.

I learn more about the vastness of Jesus when Sophie struggles to write a science paper about the creation of the moon.

I learn more about the kindness of Jesus when my children scour the neighborhood for a lost kitten.

I learn more about the gentleness of Jesus when Julia tenderly holds a roly-poly bug, naming it Alice and making her a nice bed of grass.

I learn more about the creator Jesus when I marvel at Aidan's intricate drawing of a ship.

I learn more about the joy of Jesus when Julia sings "He has been salted. The King has been salted on high. I will re-praise him." (No matter that her lyrics are different—she dances like David with all her might, with brown eyes turned heavenward.)

Can God feel the wind? I believe he does—through the cheeks of my son. And he is kind enough to let me come along for the ride.

Dear Jesus, I pray you will show me the importance of humbling myself like a little child. Instead of instructor today, help me put on the hat of "learner." Use my children, Lord, to teach me more about you. Use their words to point me to your Word. Use their freedom to infuse freedom into my heart.

9

BODIES
LIKE JENNIFERS

N THE 1830S BEING PLUMP was a fashion statement. It was a status symbol for a businessman to join the Fat Men's Club of Connecticut. Thin girls lamented in letters to the *Ladies Home Journal* that they couldn't put on weight. Some women padded their clothing so they would resemble portly stage actress Lillian Russell.

Times have changed—an enormous understatement. Now, instead of padding our clothing with pretend fat, we have real fat sucked through a hose in an attempt to look like actresses named Jennifer. All around us are images of stick women whose impossibly white teeth sport porcelain veneers. And if they happen to eat too many Twinkies? Airbrush to the rescue! Thighs shrink, busts expand with airy paint. Major women's magazines have even decapitated women—adding their smiling heads to slimmer bodies not their own.

How are we as Christian women to live in this topsy-turvy world? We can't decapitate our heads. Airbrushes don't work on three-dimensional people. How do we honor Jesus with our bodies? With the stretch marks of motherhood, the wrinkles of wisdom, and the gray hair of patience, how can we feel happy in our skin?

When I attended an *Intimate Issues* seminar presented by Lorraine Pintus and Linda Dillow, Lorraine shared a story that frightened and humbled me. She was feeling unattractive, so much so that it inhibited her desire to be touched by her husband. Frustrated, her husband took out a piece of paper and wrote the words "I praise you because I am fearfully and wonderfully made; your works are wonderful, I know that full well" (Psalm 139:14). He told her to stand in front of the mirror naked and thank God that he made her wonderfully.

What followed was a humbling time for Lorraine. As she scanned her not-so-Jennifer body, she was able to thank God for her hair, for the ability to see, for being able to hear her children sing, for the privilege of bearing children, for feet to run, and for hands that hold.

None of us have perfect bodies. That won't happen until we have our new bodies in heaven. No amount of airbrushing will perfect us on this earth. Besides, our essential beauty as women lies in the heart, not in the folds of our skin.

The most beautiful thing about this body is that it houses Beauty personified. "Do you not know that your body is a temple of the Holy Spirit, who is in you, whom you have received from God? You are not your own; you were bought at a price. Therefore honor God with your body" (1 Corinthians 6:19-20). The more we meditate on this Scripture, the more it quickens us to make our temple hospitable for the Holy One.

That means we take care of our bodies—but not to the extent that we slip into pride. We may think, *Well, I am certainly not proud of my body. I'm embarrassed. It's not even close to what I want it to be.* Simply put, we can be prideful if we revere our body or loathe it. Pride is preoccupation with self.

Instead, we ought to view our bodies realistically. Our body houses our soul. Our body reflects our character. With our body, we hug a crying child, listen to an exasperated friend, and hold our husband's hand. Our bodies are fearfully and wonderfully made—to experience pain, joy, loss, laughter, and anger. God's desire for us is to honor him with every part of us—including our body.

No matter what our culture dictates—wear padding to appear plump or have our natural padding removed—we are *always* to honor God with our bodies. Part of honoring him is honoring our children and husband. Instead of lamenting flabby upper arms today, rejoice that those arms embrace the people God has placed in your life. Rejoice that he gave you arms. Rejoice that he made you just as you are—to house the Holy Spirit and to bring hope to that large segment of the world that's dying under the strain of having to be beautiful to be loved.

Dear Jesus, thank you for making me just as I am. Help me to honor this temple you've created. Forgive me for disdaining my body. Help me to see it as you do, and help me to honor you with it. Show me who you want me to embrace today, Lord. I want to be your hands and feet in this crazy, mixed-up world.

10

BEWARE OF
MAKING VOWS

*I*N THAT CAREFREE AGE BEFORE PARENTHOOD, I used to make vows. I'd say wise things like, "I will give my children sweet cereal when they ask for it" or "I will *always* let my children choose their own books" or "I'm *never* going to say *because I said so.*" This, of course, was prior to my changing even one putrid diaper.

Now, I laugh. For a change of pace from the old standbys of Cheerios and Frosted Mini Wheats, I buy Cocoa Puffs now and again—much to the delight of my sugar-loving children. Blindly, I let my youngest choose books at the library—only to find out she brought home inappropriate ones. I monitor choices more closely now. And, yes, much to my surprise, I say *because I said so,* particularly when laundry folding is involved.

Have you made similar resolute vows, only to giggle at them later? What about deeper vows—vows that represent painful parts of your upbringing? Many of us, if we dig below the surface, parent out of rebellion. Because our family of origin injured us, we determine never to make the same mistakes.

My parents were rarely around, so I determined to be a stay-at-home mother. I didn't want my children to come home from school, locate a key under a doormat, and plop themselves alone in front of the TV. I wanted to be the June Cleaver I never had, doling out fresh chocolate chip cookies to smiling, grateful children. Because I stayed at home, I thought I had overcome my upbringing—unlike those who repeat the mistakes of their parents.

That notion was false. I am still bound to my family. I still suffer wounds. Authors Don and Jan Frank in the book *Unclaimed Baggage* poked holes in my belief that I was free from my past. People like me "are living their lives *in reaction* to the system they are still subconsciously rebelling against. As a result, they are truly not free agents but are still tied to their past in that they are reacting to it."[3]

When motherhood is marked more by a reaction to the past than by a heart for my children, I am falling short of God's design for motherhood. Reactionary living is a life lived in fear. If I parent by worrying whether or not I am damaging my children the way I was damaged, I will constantly be introspective. That introspection ends up sounding like *You're turning into your parents. You'll never measure up. Your children will wind up in counseling.*

Instead of the gentle voice of the Holy Spirit prompting us to love and cheering us even after we fail, we will constantly be living under the fear of failure. We will be ruled by our past.

How then—to paraphrase Francis Schaeffer—shall we live? It's so much better to be proactive in raising children rather than reactive. Praying through Psalm 116 is a great place to start.

Ask for God's help. Instead of compensating for your pain, cry to him to heal your heart. "I love the LORD, for he heard my voice; he heard my cry for mercy. Because he turned his ear to me, I will call on him as long as I live. The cords of death entangled me, the anguish of the grave came upon me; I was overcome by trouble and sorrow. Then I called on the name of the LORD: 'O LORD, save me!' " (verses 1-4).

Tell the truth about your pain and those who hurt you. Declare God's help in the midst of the pain. "The LORD, is gracious and righteous; our God is full of compassion. The LORD protects the simplehearted; when I was in great need, he saved me. Be at rest once more, O my soul, for the LORD has been good to you. For you, O LORD, have delivered my soul from death, my eyes from tears, my feet from stumbling, that I may walk before the LORD in the land of the living. I believed; therefore I said, 'I am greatly afflicted.' And in my dismay I said, 'All men are liars'" (verses 5-11).

Acknowledge that he is the One who has freed you. "How can I repay the LORD for all his goodness to me? I will lift up the cup of salvation and call on the name of the LORD. I will fulfill my vows to the LORD in the presence of all his people. Precious in the sight of the LORD is the death of his saints. O LORD, truly I am your servant; I am your servant, the son of your maidservant; you have freed me from my chains" (verses 12-16).

Make your vows to the Lord and for the Lord. Instead of living in fear of failure, praise him, letting him infuse your parenting. "I will sacrifice a thank offering to you and call on the name of the LORD. I will fulfill my vows to the LORD in the presence of all his people, in the courts of the house of the LORD, in your midst, O Jerusalem. Praise the LORD" (verses 17-19).

Only through God's healing, direction, and power will we be able to love our children unfettered from the worries of the past.

Dear Jesus, I pray you would help me identify where I have made unhealthy vows. Strip away my own self-sufficiency as I try to parent my children. Peel away the hurting layers of my heart. Lead me afresh into your presence so that I can make healthy vows to you, Lord.

11

The Secret
of Secrets

ENT CLOSE TO MY EAR, my five-year-old whispers, "I have a secret, Mommy!" Usually, her secret is "I love you"; sometimes it is "your Christmas present is..." Although my daughter doesn't instinctively know this, secrets are whispered because they are *meant* to be kept between two people. They are private, intimate conversations only audible to a circle of two.

Did you know God has secrets? Did you know he confides in his followers? Unfortunately, as busy mothers, we seldom stop long enough to hear his whispers. Laden by laundry, barraged by bunk beds yet unmade, disturbed by dishes, our minds are full of tasks still undone. Often there is no room for the quiet, encouraging voice of our Savior.

Searching the Scriptures, I've realized four important things about secrets:

God confides his secrets to those who fear him. "The secret of the LORD is for those who fear Him, and He will make them know His covenant" (Psalm 25:14 NASB). What does it mean to fear the Lord? Should we tremble at the thought of God? Perhaps. The connotation of fear is a hushed reverence. Think of it this way: Who would the president of the United States entrust his secrets to? A stranger walking on the White House lawn? A governor from a distant state? No, he will entrust his secrets to those he knows intimately, to those who highly regard the importance of his words—close advisors, longtime friends, a trusted spouse. God entrusts us with his secrets when we are deeply intimate with him, when we value our relationship with him above all others, when we are trustworthy to keep his secrets. Although difficult to cultivate while raising children, it's important we choose intimacy with him over busyness. That's when he whispers his secrets.

God's secrets are often his delights. Knowing his secrets means understanding what makes him joyful. Oswald Chambers expands this idea. "Many will confide to you their secret sorrows, but the last mark of intimacy is to confide secret joys. Have we ever let God tell us any of his joys?"[4] We'll tell our hairdresser about the friend who drives us batty. We'll tell a casual acquaintance that our child is making us crazy. But we reserve our joy for our most intimate friends. Those are the friends who won't balk at our good news, who will ardently rejoice in our success. Are you the kind of intimate friend God can reserve his secret joys for? Does your heart leap when he gets glory, when his will is done on earth?

God sees in secret. "When you give to the needy, do not let your left hand know what your right hand is doing, so that your giving may be in secret. Then your Father, who sees what is done in secret, will reward you" (Matthew 6:3-4). "When you pray, go into your room, close the door and pray to your Father who is unseen. Then your Father, who sees what is done in secret, will reward you" (Matthew 6:6). So much of what we experience as Christianity is outward. Television preachers have big, visible ministries. In our churches we openly pass the offering plate and offer prayer for everyone to hear. Although there's nothing inherently wrong with that, it's important to understand that the spiritual condition of our heart is unseen. God sees what we think, feel, and do in secret; therefore, we should pay close attention to our secret life. Since he sees in secret, what does he see? Our jealousies? Our inner rage? Our quiet peace? Our pessimism? We ought to cry the psalmist's prayer: "Search me, O God, and know my heart; test me and know my anxious thoughts. See if there is any offensive way in me, and lead me in the way everlasting" (Psalm 139:23-24). The God who sees in secret delights to answer that prayer.

God rewards secret things. As a mother who's stayed at home over a decade now, I would have despaired unless I knew that God sees me in my silent, secret acts of motherhood. He sees me when I pray for my children. He sees me when I watch them sleep, brushing hair from their sweaty brows. He sees every kindness and chronicles them for future reward. So much of motherhood is unseen, secret. Take heart. He sees you.

Dear Jesus, I want to be so connected with you that you tell me your secrets. I want to know what delights your heart, what brings you joy. Help me in the daily grind of motherhood to connect with you, hear your whispered secrets, and understand that you see me even as I bandage a skinned knee.

12

THE INTERCEDING SAVIOR

o get Mommy!" Julia screamed her request to Sophie, who, in turn, ran to get me.

"Julia's hurt!"

It wasn't hard to find Julia—I heard her screams three rooms away. "What's wrong?" I asked.

"Aidan pushed me, and now I'm hurt." She pointed to her bottom. Apparently they were arguing about which one would get to sit on the piano bench and he prevailed. When he pushed her off, she scraped herself on the piano bench's sharp wooden corner. She was bleeding.

Julia asked Sophie to intercede for her. Sophie ran to get me. With my husband, Patrick, I cleaned up her wound, determined if she needed stitches (she didn't), and held her until she calmed down. This is the essence of intercession.

The fascinating thing to me is that we have an interceding God. When we are wounded, we can, through the Holy Spirit, ask Jesus to run to the Father on our behalf. We can be assured that the Father listens to Jesus—and that the Father will come to our rescue, clean our wounds, determine if we need extra care, and hold us until we calm down. With this in view, let's consider a few things.

Consider the Mediator. "Who is he that condemns? Christ Jesus, who died—more than that, who was raised to life—is at the right hand of God and is also interceding for us" (Romans 8:34). Jesus Christ the God-man is at the right hand of God praying for us! He is not begrudging us. He is not tired of our prayers. He does not say, "Oh, it's you again." He is infinitely more patient with us. We may tire of our children's demands, but he does not tire of ours. He responds to us as if we were all screaming, needy Julias.

Consider the Spirit. "He who searches our hearts knows the mind of the Spirit, because the Spirit intercedes for the saints in accordance with God's will" (Romans 8:27). How amazing that even when my heart doesn't comprehend God's will, the Spirit does, and he intercedes for me accordingly. Julia didn't know anything about her condition. She just knew she was hurting. Because I am her mother, I was able to ascertain exactly what she needed in the moment.

Consider his occupation. "Therefore he is able to save completely those who come to God through him, because he always lives to intercede for them" (Hebrews 7:25). Jesus *lives* to intercede for us. It's his work on the cross that enables us to approach God the Father. It's his job to save us completely, 24 hours a day, seven days a week. He never rests. Just as Julia knew that if she called for me, I'd come running, we should realize that God is always available to intercede on our behalf.

The New Testament uses two Greek words for intercession. In the above three references the transliterated word is *entugchano,* which means to light upon a person or fall in with. It connotes meeting a person for the purpose of conversation, consultation, or supplication. At its basic level, it means to pray or entreat.

What a beautiful picture of intercession. It's not merely Jesus praying on our behalf; it's his willingness to walk with us, to light upon us, to fall in with us in the midst of our mothering. Jesus wants to meet with us. He wants to talk to us. He wants us to consult him.

There is another word for intercession: *huperentugchano*. This word has just one meaning: to intercede for one. "In the same way, the Spirit helps us in our weakness. We do not know what we ought to pray for, but the Spirit himself intercedes *[huperentugchano]* for us with groans that words cannot express" (Romans 8:26). This is a comfort for me when I am feeling alone; Jesus will intercede just for me. In the midst of a chaotic house and fighting children, all I can do sometimes is say, "Jesus!" When grief knocks on my door, all I can do is groan. Even in that, I am praying. Even without words, the Holy Spirit is translating *my* gibberish and angst and sending it to the throne room of God. C.S. Lewis addressed this holy translation in a poem he wrote entitled "A Footnote to All Prayers." The last couplet reads:

> "Take not, O Lord, our literal sense. Lord, in Thy great,
> Unbroken speech our limping metaphor translate."[5]

The Holy Spirit takes my ramblings, groanings, and meanderings and presents them purely to the heavens. It would be the same if Julia just screamed and didn't ask Sophie to get me. Still, Sophie would understand the need and run to me anyway. And I would run to rescue Julia.

Lord, thank you that you live to intercede for me. Help me to understand your amazing availability. I praise you for translating my words into heavenly prayers that reach your throne. In the midst of a busy life, enable me to remember your nearness and help me to model that nearness to my children.

13

THE ENTROPY MONSTER

SOMEWHERE IN THE BACK of my tired mommy brain, I remember something I learned in college. I remember learning about entropy. I remember the professor telling us that entropy was about a system or a universe moving from a state of order to disorder. I don't know why, but the definition stuck, filed neatly behind "don't mix ammonia and bleach" in my brain's useful-information-if-I-am-ever-on-Jeopardy drawer.

Entropy is a malevolent force, bent on cluttering my home. The Entropy Monster puts my five-year-old's teeny-tiny underwear in *my* laundry basket, mocking my wider frame. He dirties dishes and lets them sit and sit and sit until they are steel-encrusted. He takes every toy out of every toy box and flings those toys to the four corners of the house, all the while laughing. He adds more rings to the toilet bowls, puts more bills in the mailbox, and loses invoices. He stays up late at night and puts rat's nests in my sleeping daughters' hair. He loves Legos. He puts them everywhere—in the fridge, in the pathway of my tender feet, and, apparently, in Julia's stomach. He steals the two of clubs from our deck of cards.

The Entropy Monster is also at work in my heart. Though I'd love to say I am becoming more a follower of Christ every day, that wouldn't always be truthful. My spiritual life can spin from a state of order to disorder in one 24-hour period—from spending diligent, meaningful times with Jesus to not thinking one thought about him all day. Life's craziness beckons me to mini-crises all day long, so that instead of communing with Jesus like Brother Lawrence, I am running bedraggled by Father Time.

To eradicate the Entropy Monster's grip on your heart, or at least loosen his grip, try the following strategies.

Confound the Entropy Monster by storing up treasures he cannot touch. He cannot reach beyond the grave. The treasures you store up there will never decay. "Do not store up for yourselves treasures on earth, where moth and rust destroy, and where thieves break in and steal. But store up for yourselves treasures in heaven, where moth and rust do not destroy, and where thieves do not break in and steal. For where your treasure is, there your heart will be also" (Matthew 6:19-21). Everything we do for Jesus, even kissing our children's boo-boos, is chronicled by him. Our lives may feel chaotic, but if we are constantly endeavoring to store up eternal treasures, Entropy cannot spoil them.

Believe that God is making you new every day. Despite our tendency to fall apart spiritually, we have an incredible, always-available Savior who renews us with the dawn. "Therefore we do not lose heart. Thought outwardly we are wasting away, yet inwardly we are being renewed day by day. For our light and momentary troubles are achieving for us an eternal glory that far outweighs them all" (2 Corinthians 4:16-17).

Fix your eyes on the unseen. Entropy is all around us, beckoning us to attend every mess, every drama, every heartache. It's what Charles Hummel called "the tyranny of the urgent." Instead, determine to fix your spiritual eyes on what is not seen. "We fix our eyes not on what is seen, but on what is unseen. For what is seen is temporary, but what is unseen is eternal" (2 Corinthians 4:18).

Let Jesus' strength be what pulls you through an entropy-filled life. If we constantly are running the treadmill of life in our own exhaustive strength, either we will exult when we win (and become prideful) or we will cry when we fall. We are to live in such a way that others see Jesus in us. "But we have this treasure in jars of clay to show that this all-surpassing power is from God and not from us" (2 Corinthians 4:7).

Entropy happens. Life and its chaos rub off on us. And yet we have inexhaustible resources in Jesus Christ, who called himself Living Water. His strength does not abate. His joy is complete. His healing waters flow freely. And someday, when we meet him face-to-face, we will no longer be held hostage by Entropy's clutches. Dancing on streets of gold, celebrating the God of life, we will never again have to face decay or death or disorder.

Lord, help me to understand that entropy happens in this life. When it does, I pray you'd lift my gaze to you. Help me to store up treasures in heaven where decay cannot erode them. Enable me to walk through my day today with a heart bent toward you. Thank you for the reality of heaven. May its existence spill over into the way I love my family.

14

To Wonder
at Roly-Polies

Y YOUNGEST DAUGHTER is fascinated by roly-polies—those little black bugs that roll into a ball when you touch them. "They crawl like a little pig," she says as she stoops low to the ground, petting their armored backs.

"They're so very cute." Julia captures the poor things, inevitably separating for eternity spouses, siblings, star-crossed roly-poly lovers, and best friends. She especially likes to place them in lidded jars, giving them a stout diet of twigs, dirt, and grass.

As I watch her interact with these tiny creatures, I am struck by how little I wonder—about a little black bug or a crimson-pink sunset or a warm breeze in winter. Because my grown-up existence is surrounded by gas bills, Cheerio-laden kitchen floors, and children who like to be fed at dinnertime, I seldom take time out of my life to wonder at the beauty of this world, nor do I stoop, low to the ground, to contemplate the majesty of God in a roly-poly.

The *Oxford Illustrated Dictionary* defines wonder as "surprise mingled with admiration or curiosity."[6] Doesn't that aptly describe a child's view of life? Perhaps that's why Jesus promoted a child's-eye view of the kingdom of God. "I tell you the truth, unless you change and become like little children, you will never enter the kingdom of heaven. Therefore whoever humbles himself like this child is the greatest in the kingdom of heaven" (Matthew 18:3-4).

It's hard for me to wrap my mind around Jesus' words, particularly because I don't remember ever being a child. Because of circumstances in my upbringing, I grew up quickly—a responsible adult in a child's body. I don't know how to wonder at a roly-poly. I don't know how to capture life through the lens of a five-year-old. I don't know how to just rest and watch a bird alight on a branch—not when dishes beckon.

Still, I sense his calling. I hear his voice. "Become like Julia," Jesus tells me. "Wonder. Contemplate. Be fascinated."

I am reminded of King David, who learned obedience as a child under a vast tent of stars. David spent his childhood considering the wonder of God. Later, as a psalmist-king, he wrote about his wonder: "O Lord, our Lord, how majestic is your name in all the earth! You have set your glory above the heavens. From the lips of children and infants you have ordained praise because of your enemies, to silence the foe and the avenger. When I consider your heavens, the work of your fingers, the moon and the stars, which you have set in place, what is man that you are mindful of him, the son of man that you care for him?" (Psalm 8:1-4).

I am reminded of Mary, the mother of Jesus, who treasured things in her heart. She paused to be amazed. She stopped long enough to consider the paradoxical truth that she birthed God in the flesh. Like a child, she wondered.

I am reminded of the people who witnessed a crippled man leaping. "They recognized him as the same man who used to sit begging at the temple gate called Beautiful, and they were filled with wonder and amazement at what had happened to him" (Acts 3:10). The Greek word for wonder here is *thambos*. It means to render immovable, to dumbfound. When was the last time I was rendered immovable by wonder?

I can easily rationalize my lack of wonderment. *Well, I'd wonder too if I were King David. If I carried the Son of God in my womb, I'd pause and consider it. If a lame man suddenly leapt to his feet, sure, I'd be dumbstruck. But life today? There's nothing to wonder about.*

There would be if I took Jesus' words seriously…*become a child.* The world from a thigh-high perspective is full of God's beauty; I simply need to shorten myself. For the sake of my relationship with God, I must stoop, low to the ground, and consider the roly-poly. I must choose to pull away from the tasks of motherhood and consider the heavens. I must sit cross-legged on the grass and wonder at the songs of birds in the trees overhead or the shape of clouds trailing the sky or the sound of children's laughter. All of these point to the Creator. All of these are his paintings. All of these require wonder.

May it be that we don't get so caught up in the duties of motherhood that we forget to wonder like the children he's entrusted to us.

Jesus, you tell me to come into your kingdom as a child, but so often I see the world through cynical adult lenses. Refocus my heart, Lord. Make me attune to wonder today. Teach me to stop and consider your heavens, your creatures, and your incarnation. I want to wonder, Lord.

15

NATIVE HABITAT

OUR CHILDREN GREW RESTLESS when we stayed late at a friend's house. Sophie, then five, sighed, "C'mon, Mommy and Daddy. I need to get back to my native habitat."

Sophie wanted to go home. When fatigue or bewilderment sets in, we long for the place where life makes sense, where we can rest from the cares of this world. Perhaps you've heard the phrase "Heaven is my home." God created us, according to author Randy Alcorn, for a person and a place. That person is Jesus. That place is heaven. In order to live lives that impact eternity, we need to be living for our native habitat—heaven.

Have you considered heaven? There have been many times I've not wanted to think about it. I'd rather focus on the here and now, my home here on earth. But now that I understand more about the place I will live for eternity, I ask for heaven.

What is heaven?

I've created an acrostic: HEAVEN. Heaven is...

A **H**abitat for the righteous. Jesus, the Carpenter and Creator of the Universe, is preparing a home for you right now (John 14:1-3). Because of what Jesus did on the cross, we, if we have given our lives to him in repentance, can live in heaven for eternity.

"Praise be to the God and Father of our Lord Jesus Christ! In his great mercy he has given us new birth into a living hope through the resurrection of Jesus Christ from the dead, and into an inheritance that can never perish, spoil, or fade—kept in heaven for you" (1 Peter 1:3-4).

*E*ternally worshipful. "Then I heard every creature in heaven and on earth and under the earth and on the sea, and all that is in them, singing: 'To him who sits on the throne and to the Lamb be praise and honor and glory and power for ever and ever!'" (Revelation 5:13). Have you ever been so caught up in worship that you feel you've tasted heaven? That's just a tiny glimpse of heavenly worship. Worship is our primary occupation in heaven. Since that is true, what are you doing now to prepare for this important job? How are you worshiping as you parent your children?

A *place of reward.* Not only do we have a home in heaven and hearts to worship unashamedly, but we will be rewarded. "We must all appear before the judgment seat of Christ, that each one may receive what is due him for the things done while in the body, whether good or bad" (2 Corinthians 5:10). Every cup of cool water offered to our children, every prayer uttered in silence, every tear shed for the lost, every resource given to the Lord's causes—all these are chronicled by him.

Where God is **V***ictorious and just.* Living in a fallen world, we long for justice. There will be a day when God will right every wrong. He will perfectly judge as he lays everything bare. Revelation 20:11-15 details this last judgment culminating with, "If anyone's name was not found written in the book of life, he was thrown into the lake of fire" (verse 15). This should cause us to realize every person God places in our midst has a future—either in heaven or hell.

E*arthlike in some of its attributes.* There is feasting. There is wine. There are streets. There are animals. Heaven is not a state of nothingness—it's a place like earth but light-years better. In *The Last Battle* C.S. Lewis explains this paradox. "I have come home at last! This is my real country! I belong here. This is the land I have been looking for all my life, though I never knew it till now. The reason why we loved the old Narnia is that it sometimes looked a little like this one."[7]

No place like home. Heaven may resemble earth or have traits of earth, but it is no place like earth. There will be things missing. "He will wipe every tear from their eyes. There will be no more death or mourning or crying or pain, for the old order of things has passed away" (Revelation 21:4). Someday, in our home, our cries will be stilled by the sweet presence of Jesus.

In *Mere Christianity* C.S. Lewis articulated, "Aim at heaven and you will get earth 'thrown in.' Aim at earth and you will get neither."[8] Amid the crying of little ones, the busyness of tasks, and the harried pace by which we run, we forget heaven. As mothers we need to aim there—our native habitat—as we maintain our own homes.

Lord, forgive me for aiming at earth. I don't want to be shortsighted. I long to have an eternal perspective and a heart bent toward eternal things. I want to long for heaven. Place in me that longing.

16

LOVING
LITTLE SINNERS

Clee

IDAN PROVIDED MY HUSBAND and me an interesting view into a sinner's mastermind. He pulled the bait-and-switch tactic, asking me whether he could have a sleepover after Patrick had already said no. He was disappointed that we messed up his plans. In the midst of this disappointment, he didn't seem to realize his error.

"Why did you ask *me* when you knew Daddy already said no?" I asked.

Tears pooled in his large eyes. "I accidentally did it on purpose," he cried.

There's a lot of accidentally-did-it-on-purpose at our house. Of course, it's much easier to point to my children's sins than to face my own selfishness. The fact is, I want to do things my way, in my timing, for my benefit. I accidentally do things on purpose. I accidentally ignore my children while I write. I accidentally yell when I should stop and be quiet. I accidentally shun my husband's advances when I'm tired.

God asks me, "Why did you do that when I already told you no?"

Tears pool in my aging eyes. "Well, er, I accidentally did it on purpose."

Thankfully, the Lord extends grace to me when I repent. He visits me anew when I dare to confess my sins to my children and husband. I see him more clearly in my humility and my family's extension of grace and love.

In the midst of my sinning and theirs, my children offer me great words of wisdom—the type of wisdom uncanny for youngsters and maddeningly difficult to heed. One afternoon Sophie ran from her room, took a deep breath, and told me, "I love Aidan even when he comes in my room and sins." Upon further investigation, I discovered Aidan, then a toddler, had upset her tea set, sending it crashing to the floor.

Sophie understood love. Even when Aidan had blatant disregard for tea parties set up on doll-sized tables, she forgave him. She methodically set the table again—with correct silverware placement—and told Aidan not to do that again. I'm sure he did.

Our home is a haven for sinners, small and big. We upset each other's tea sets daily (and sometimes hourly). Our home is also a microcosm of the world. It's our training ground for learning to love and forgive. It's the place of our biggest failures and should be the place where the biggest doses of grace are extended. The key is to provide an environment where failure is allowed.

How can we do that? By following James' advice: "Confess your sins to each other and pray for each other so that you may be healed. The prayer of a righteous man is powerful and effective" (James 5:16).

Confess your sins. Children learn more by observing us than by our didactic preaching. We must model acknowledging our own sin. I've found that when aggravation between my children and me escalates, I can stop the escalation and invite love by saying, "Hey, Mommy blew it. Will you forgive me?" My confession stops the hype, quieting my children. Perhaps because they are keenly aware of their own failings, they readily forgive me. When they admit their sins, I hope I am the Father waiting on tiptoes at the end of the lane—the Father who eagerly awaits his prodigal to return home. May it be that I embrace and forgive my children as they have embraced and forgiven me.

Pray for each other. Not only should we model humility, we must also model prayer. When stress or pain or discord bewitch our home, only prayer dissolves the tyranny. In prayer we are blessedly humble before our children, acknowledging that we don't have all the answers and that we need God's presence to pull us through.

Welcome healing and believe God will accomplish it. Families are famous for locking themselves into destructive patterns. If we confess our sins and pray for each other, God has the opportunity to break the cycle. He can only do that, though, when we are broken.

Like a tea set upset, our families are in a state of breaking and rebuilding, of upsetting and resetting. We accidentally sin on purpose. In order to move forward, we must echo Sophie's sentiment. *I love you even when you come into my life and sin.*

Dear Jesus, help me to extend grace to my children and husband today. Show me where I am accidentally sinning on purpose. Give me the wherewithal to confess my sins before my family. Teach me to pray. Help me believe you will heal us.

17

I Cast All
My Kids upon You

WHEN SOPHIE WAS FOUR years old, she misunderstood the words to the famous praise chorus, "I cast all my cares upon you." Instead she bellowed, "I cast all my kids upon you."

How appropriate for mothers today. To fully understand that everything and every person in our life is a gift from God is to cast everything at his feet. I have a friend who can't seem to do that. She so longs to prevent accidents in her children's lives that she won't let them ride in cars with other parents. She won't let her children explore the world—not without her around. She's afraid. She worries about things that *might* happen to her children; consequently, she is bound up in fear.

We must cast our children at the feet of Jesus. He made them. He knows them. He loves them a billion times more than we can fathom. We often read Romans 8:38-39 as if those verses were exclusively for us. We forget that God loves our children in like manner. "I am convinced that neither death nor life, neither angels nor demons, neither the present nor the future, nor any powers, neither height nor depth, nor anything else in all creation, will be able to separate us from the love of God that is in Christ Jesus our Lord."

We hold on to these gifts—our children whom God loves—and believe that we possess them. Essentially, we act as if we own our children.

When we were working toward going overseas to plant churches, we received email from our team leader detailing how their eldest child was getting harassed almost every day. Obviously, we fretted for our own children because in one year they'd be in the same situation. If we had not first cast our children at his feet, we'd be apt to avoid the call on our lives.

American parents seem to believe that a parent's primary role is protection. Sure, we are to take care of our children and prevent harm when possible. Children, however, aren't harm proof. If we live under the illusion that we can somehow prevent their pain, we will live life like my friend—with great fear. And if we cushion them from every bit of life's pain and consequences, we rob them of becoming decision-making adults. Every decision we make for our children is a decision they cannot make.

Does it agonize me that my children may be injured in school? Of course. I have to cast them at his feet, along with a crib full of fears. I sometimes equate fear with love—even though doing that contradicts 1 John 4:18: "The one who fears is not made perfect in love." If you are having difficulty casting your children at his feet, consider the following verses.

"When I am afraid, I will trust in you. In God, whose word I praise, in God I trust; I will not be afraid. What can mortal man do to me?" (Psalm 56:3-4). God will take care of our children. He is infinitely stronger than mere man.

"Have I not commanded you? Be strong and courageous. Do not be terrified; do not be discouraged, for the LORD your God will be with you wherever you go" (Joshua 1:9). Not only will God be there for us as we mother our children, he will be with our children when they are out of eyeshot. He will be our children's constant companion.

"God is our refuge and strength, an ever-present help in trouble. Therefore we will not fear, though the earth give way and the mountains fall into the heart of the sea, though its waters roar and foam and the mountains quake with their surging" (Psalm 46:1-3). Life may fall apart. We may fall apart. Our children may fall apart. Yet God promises he will be with us, ever-present.

"Do not fear, for I am with you; do not be dismayed, for I am your God. I will strengthen you and help you; I will uphold you with my righteous right hand" (Isaiah 41:10). Not only will the Lord give us strength in our feebleness, but he will also strengthen our children to face the world.

"Therefore do not worry about tomorrow, for tomorrow will worry about itself. Each day has enough trouble of its own" (Matthew 6:34). As mothers, we often fret about our children's future, yet God holds their future just as he holds the future of the world.

As Sophie sang, we must cast all our kids upon him—leaving our fears, worries, and insecurities at his feet. The Lord is more than capable to shoulder our fretting, and as a gentle Shepherd, he will cherish and love our children far better than we can.

Dear Jesus, I worry about my children. I am bound up in fear for them. Help me to cast them all at your feet today, knowing that you love them more than I can. Teach me to give you all my fears—every day.

18

CHOOSING TRINKETS
OVER TREASURES

M Y CHILDREN LIVE FOR ALLOWANCE DAY. As
quick as I am quick to forget, they are equally as quick to remind
me. Five glorious dollars—five crisp bills. You'd think something
as benign as a dirty green piece of paper would make them turn
their noses up. No, to them, money is power—power to buy
trinkets. Once the initial allowance nagging is over, the Dollar
Store pestering begins. "Please, Mommy, take me to the Dollar
Store. I promise I'll clean my room every day for a year. Puhhh-
lease?"

Usually I relent, but not without a firm reminder that one of
the dollars goes to Jesus, and that they'd surely be able to buy the
latest turbo-charged Bionicle if they'd just cram the rest of their
money in their piggy banks. But, inevitably, the allure of plastic
removable head Barbie dolls, camouflaged army men, and balsa
snap-together planes win over their capricious hearts. Five days
later, headless Barbies, casualty-bound army men hunkering
down in couch cushions and shoes, and balsa plane crashes
remind me that trinkets are transitory.

It's easy to point the finger at childish purchases. It's easy to
overlook the lesson God may have for us down the aisles of the

local Dollar Store. How often do I settle for the here and now, the transitory illusions of life? How often do I rush to fill my heart with trinkets like television, food, shopping, the Internet, or movies while the true Treasure, Jesus Christ, stands to the side? The truth is, trinkets never satisfy. We've duped ourselves into believing that *this* time a new outfit will fill us, that *this* time our children's accomplishments will satisfy the longings of our hearts. Only God can fill our deepest longings. Only his treasures last forever.

The apostle Paul knew our own propensity to chase after worldly trinkets. In 2 Corinthians 4:18, he pulls back the curtains of time and eternity and casts light on our backward thinking. He encourages, "We fix our eyes not on what is seen, but on what is unseen. For what is seen is temporary, but what is unseen is eternal."

Like Peter taking tentative steps on a path of water, gawking at the waves, we become distracted by temporary trinkets and start to sink. Jesus beckoned Peter to walk, to look into his eyes, but the reality of waves licking his feet made him miss the treasure of Jesus, at least temporarily.

Like Martha, serving her friends with a haughty spirit, we frenetically serve the God who praises the quiet one, the one sitting at his feet. Serving our children without first sitting at his feet is a temporary trinket, soon cast aside. The Treasure—the Unseen One—and our passionate relationship with him—these are eternal.

What do you spend your life on? Do you rush to the spiritual Dollar Store to stock your coffers with trinkets that merely fill this life temporarily? There are times I think a new outfit will make me ultimately happy. I've chased after completing to-do lists that never get done, thinking that if I could just cross off one more task, I'd be fulfilled. I've coveted other people's homes, believing if I just had one more bedroom, I'd be satisfied. Yet nothing—no outfit, no crossed off to-do list, no house—can fill my heart like Jesus can. He is my true treasure.

Like marauders on Fat Tuesday who don strings and strings of apparent jewels, we parade around our trinkets, thinking them beautiful and worthy of our time and attention. The problem is, Wednesday always comes. Street sweepers and bulldozers push these "jewels" into heaps, intermingled with garbage and broken glass. Scoop after scoop is sent to the landfill—the once-thought treasure becoming trash. At the end of time, our trinkets will be sent to the landfill. The Treasure of our life—Jesus—will ask us to give an account. That's when we'll know when we've walked the spiritual Dollar Store aisle, living for things that don't remain.

The next time you reattach a headless Barbie, reconvene scattered army men, or glue the wing back on a balsa plane, remember to choose the eternal things—Jesus Christ, the children he created, and the words of his Book.

Lord, help me to live for you, my true Treasure. Show me today the trinkets I pursue, whether they are tangible, like the latest fashions or furniture or a new minivan, or intangible, like status or pride or having control. I don't want to live for trinkets. I want to live for what will last forever in heaven, that place where moth and rust can't touch. I want to live for you.

19

BEARING THE COST

A FAVORITE ALLEGORY OF MINE is *Hinds' Feet on High Places* by Hannah Hurnard. It centers on a character named Much Afraid and her harrowing journey to the High Places of God where healing is promised by her Shepherd. After much trial and suffering, Much Afraid tries to climb an impossible precipice. During a brief respite, she spies a lone flower bursting through the craggy surface where no vegetation had been before. She asks the flower its name.

"My name is Bearing the Cost, but some call me Forgiveness."[9]

Much Afraid inquires how the flower got to that strange place.

Bearing the Cost replies, "I was separated from all my companions, exiled from home, carried here and imprisoned in this rock. It was not my choice, but the work of others who, when they had dropped me here, went away and left me to bear the results of what they had done."[10]

Isn't that what it feels like when someone you love has wronged you? When I've been wronged, I feel as if I have been plucked from my current circumstance and dropped with a thud into a dark crevasse. It's not my fault I was dropped there, but I still must live in that darkness.

As I try to bear the cost, I am learning the art of rejoicing when things seem dark. It is that darkness that harkens me to seek the Light. Like a ship's captain straining to see a beacon in a storm, I am stretching to see God's light in the midst of my tempests. The joy is that he makes himself be found. The desolation of my circumstance helps me to see only him.

When I consider my place in the clefts of my unchosen rock, I have to remember the One who truly bears the cost—Jesus. Since he was and is God, he obviously had the quality of omniscience (knowing everything) as he walked the earth. That being true, he knew about Peter's denials before he met Peter. He knew everyone would abandon him. He knew Judas would betray him. He knew the disciples would sleep as he prayed. He knew all the evil intentions of each disciple's heart—the petty jealousies, the bickering, the clamoring for recognition.

Even so, he chose to call the motley Twelve. He chose to pour his life into them for three years. I don't think any of us, knowing ahead of time that someone would deeply wound us, would choose to carry on in that relationship. Jesus did because he embodied forgiveness even before he became our sacrifice on the cross. During his agony when he bore the cost for our sins, he spoke forgiveness. Today, at the right hand of the Father, he still chooses us, knowing full well our past sins, our sins today, and our eventual sins.

If Jesus did that, knowing he would endure ridicule and abandonment by some of his followers, then shouldn't it logically follow that we should strive to do the same? If we want to have Christ-honoring homes, we must forgive as Jesus did and be merciful to those who have wounded us unintentionally or intentionally. Has someone hurt you? Has their sin put you in a place of loneliness? Do you have to bear the consequence of someone else's sin?

The slogan "What would Jesus do?" takes on a completely different meaning in the context of forgiveness. If Jesus forgives us, who are we to declare we are too hurt to forgive our neighbor, our children, our spouse, our parents? We must recognize how much we smack of the unmerciful servant in Matthew 18:21-35, who is forgiven millions but begrudges pennies. The master said to him, "You wicked servant. I canceled all that debt of yours because you begged me to. Shouldn't you have had mercy on your fellow servant just as I had on you?" (verses 32-33). Like Much Afraid, we must *bear the cost* of other's sins and forgive.

I once heard it said, "Forgiveness is giving up all hope of having a different past." The truth is, we all are named Bearing the Cost. We are all grieving our pasts and nursing old wounds. We cannot change what others have done to us, but we can change our hearts toward those same people. In that, we become more and more like Jesus—the ultimate Forgiver.

Lord, I want to forgive, but it's so hard. I've been plucked away and shoved into a rocky hole by someone else. I can't seem to see my way out. Thank you for knowing every part of me and still dying for me, still forgiving me. Help me to mete out forgiveness as you have meted it out to me—freely, joyfully, enthusiastically. Give me a forgiving heart—in my home with my spouse and my children, and in this crazy world. Help me remember that you are with me as I bear the cost of someone else's sin.

20

Children,
Our Coaches

OPHIE IS IN THE MIDST of basketball practice as I write this. Donning spanking new basketball shorts and a bright yellow T-shirt, she patiently waits for her turn at dribbling a drill. A confirmed lefty, she has a little difficulty in the world of righties. Maybe I should tell the coach. Nah, she seems so alive, so buoyant. I don't want to interrupt her rhythm, her abandon to the sport.

She's guarding now. Hands raised, skipping horizontally, she tries to get the elusive orange ball. She doesn't get it this time, but she is still smiling.

She seems taller somehow, and her eyes register more wisdom than last year. When she drops the ball, she giggles. When she makes a basket, she jumps and gives the air some high fives. At ten, she knows the oft-elusive art of resilience. I wish I could bounce back with a smile as she does.

Today, on the day of Sophie's practice, Aidan turns seven. He celebrates by sitting beside me playing with his new Legos. He can make more spaceship noises than I could ever dream up, and he seems content just being next to me creating suitable cars for alien folk.

Julia says, "Aidan, I am glad it's your birthday," and he nods. He revels in celebrations, much like Sophie revels in learning a new sport.

"Mommy, look at this guy. Look what he can do. Mommy, look at this spaceship, isn't it cool?" I nod while he continues conquering alien Lego adversaries.

Julia watches Sophie from time to time. She once told us she wanted to be a cheerleader when she grew up, which seems to fit her. She is all about encouraging others. When Sophie makes a basket, she leaps into the air and exclaims, "Hooray for Sophie! Hooray for Sophie!" She cheers for me too. "Those are good cookies you made, Mommy. Great job."

So what's the point of this existential rambling at basketball practice? Simply this: Children teach us things. Life's pace is relentless, and if we allow its speed to usurp our pause and reflection mechanism, then we miss out on its treasures.

Sophie, alert and positive, reminds me today to try new things. If I drop the ball, it's no big deal. I simply need to pick it up and dribble, laughing and hopeful. I can't learn new things if I don't risk. From her, I learn the elusive art of dusting myself off and moving on, smile in tow. She's the capricious embodiment of Philippians 3:13-14: "One thing I do: Forgetting what is behind and straining forward toward what is ahead, I press on toward the goal to win the prize for which God has called me heavenward in Christ Jesus."

Aidan educates me about the details of life. To make a spaceship come together, I need to attend to the intricacies of its form. Similarly, life has intricacies, and in those intricacies I learn life's essence. If I only see the whole, I will miss the beauty of the detail. Aidan reminds me that God is interested in the smallest flower as well as the tiniest perplexities of my life and that he is *able* to accomplish what worries me: "Why do you worry about clothes? See how the lilies of the field grow. They do not labor or spin. Yet I tell you that not even Solomon in all his splendor was dressed like one of these. If that is how God clothes the grass of the field, which is here today and tomorrow is thrown into the fire, will he not much more cloth you, O you of little faith?" (Matthew 6:28-30).

Julia has taught me the supreme gift of encouragement. Life is gray without encouraging voices. Like her, I want to bounce and jump for those who see life in shades of gray. Like her, I want to cheerlead. Some days I just need to see her encouraging smile and cheer-filled hugs. The key is not to merely long for someone to cheer me, but to look outside myself and be a Julia to someone else. I find myself more alive when I give, and at five years old, Julia has already learned that truth. She is energized when she encourages and seems to live Galatians 6:9: "Let us not become weary in doing good, for at the proper time we will reap a harvest if we do not give up."

Sophie's ponytail bobs up and down to the rhythm of her left-handed basketball skip, Aidan's spaceship flies effortlessly (and with authentic noise) at the hand of its creator, and Julia jumps up and down and cheers for them both. I am rich indeed to have them as my coaches for life.

Lord, help me to be humble enough to let my children coach me. Show me today the spiritual lessons you have for me written in the personalities of each child. I want to hear your voice and direction through their laughing, Lord.

21

Confess It to the Little People

I HAD TO CONFESS MY SINS to my children last night. Yesterday was one of those crabby mommy days where everything my children did irritated me. Julia whined and whined until I thought my eardrums would implode. Aidan sat on her little frame, practically smothering her. Sophie gave me the rolled-eyed "whatever" look when I asked her to help me with the dishes. "It's not fair" reverberated off the walls of our home. Instead of heeding the mommy's creed: "A gentle answer turns away wrath, but a harsh word stirs up anger" (Proverbs 15:1), I stirred up anger by spewing harsh words.

I knew I had crossed the line between gentle corrector and wicked disciplinarian when my son stopped mid-sentence in the kitchen and started to cry.

"What's wrong, Aidan?"

His chest heaved in and out. He sucked in his breath while a drippy tear spilled on his shirt. "Do you want to get rid of us?"

I hugged him, ashamed. The gifts God had given me—my three children—thought that I viewed them as burdens, not delights. *Forgive me, Lord.*

"Come here." I corralled all of them. We huddled together in Sophie's bedroom. "I have something to say. I didn't have patience with you today, and I am really, really sorry. I hope you can find it in your hearts to forgive me."

Sophie said, "Of course, Mommy."

"I forgive you." Julia hugged me as she said it.

Aidan, the joker boy, traced a maze pattern on his chest because I used the words "find it in your heart."

"I'm looking for the forgiveness." He pushed his finger up and down, back and forth until it stopped square in the middle of his chest. "There. Okay. I found my forgiveness. I forgive you."

I hugged the three and felt much lighter. It is a wonderful thing to confess our sins to Jesus. He promises he will forgive us and clean us up too. But it is an amazing thing to take repentance a step further—perhaps the hardest step of all—and confess our sins to our children.

I grew up in a home where adults seldom admitted fault. Even when I knew a parent was in the wrong, I'd be blamed for their inappropriate reaction. I grew up thinking I was horrible—that I caused all outbursts in my home. That type of home helped me develop an overactive conscience—where I'd take the blame for anything and everything, even when I did nothing wrong. It has crossed over into my relationship with Jesus, where I seldom feel worthy of his delight or love. I am keenly aware of my failure. Because I felt I was a bumbling disappointment, I have a hard time understanding forgiveness and grace.

So, when our children reached ages where they could understand what I was saying—and even before that time—I made it a practice to confess my shortcomings and sins to them. I didn't want them to grow up thinking they were bumbling disappointments. I wanted them to be able to grasp (instead of struggle with) God's grace and forgiveness.

Besides that, I knew that it was good for my soul to acknowledge my sin publicly. In David's confession in Psalm 51, he recognizes that putting on a religious show while not confessing sin was an abomination to God: "You do not delight in sacrifice, or I would bring it; you do not take pleasure in burnt offerings. The sacrifices of God are a broken spirit; a broken and contrite heart, O God, you will not despise" (Psalm 51:16-17).

How beautiful that the Lord simply wants our broken, incapable hearts. He longs for us to come into the light with our sin, even if it means confessing it to the little people in our lives. A side benefit of parental confession is de-escalation. The voices in our house may be in angry crescendo, but when I confess, loud shouts turn to quiet forgiveness.

Besides de-escalation, confession is good for our heart; it ensures that our heart finds the mercy it needs. It helps our heart from becoming hard and unwieldy. "He who conceals his sins does not prosper, but whoever confesses and renounces them finds mercy. Blessed is the man who always fears the LORD, but he who hardens his heart falls into trouble" (Proverbs 28:13-14).

Lord, I've often thought that a well-controlled home is pleasing to you, but there have been times when my words are too controlling, my voice too barky. Forgive me, Lord. Help me to dare confess my sins to my children. Reveal the gift of your forgiveness through their sweet voices.

22

COPYCAT ME

I ASKED OUR YOUNGEST DAUGHTER Julia what she wanted to be when she grew up—a dangerous question. Her response? "I want to be a marshmallow. And I want to be a car driver like Mommy."

Although I chuckled at Julia's desire to be a confection, I realized that much of my motherly life is spent behind the wheel of a fully functional—and not very cool—minivan. Actually, I asked her this question while driving to the post office in an attempt to soothe the quarreling mayhem erupting from the back seat.

Whether I'm a carpooling mom or an errand-running mom, I am thankful for Julia's comment, not so much that she equates motherhood with automobile maneuvering, but that she wants to be like me. Lately, I've asked her again the what-do-you-want-to-be-when-you-grow-up question. Her response was similar.

"I want to be a teacher like Miss Wilson—and a mommy like you."

Much of parenthood is imitation. I may strain to speak words of wisdom until I am pink in the face, and yet what my children remember is me—my reactions, my actions, my inaction. They by nature are copycats. Little eyes watch me all the time. When I yell, they learn that yelling gets things done. When I pout, they push out lower lips, hoping to sway me to their desires. When I laugh at Julia's Sharpie-penned body, they learn how to diffuse stress in a positive way.

Like unsuspecting sting victims on an FBI surveillance tape, I often don't realize I am being watched. It's a scary thought that my children will, after observing me, imitate my behavior. I feel quite inadequate as a mentor because I know the inclination of my heart is bent toward sin. Yet, even the apostle Paul told others to imitate him: "Even though you have ten thousand guardians in Christ, you do not have many fathers, for in Christ Jesus I became your father through the gospel. Therefore I urge you to imitate me" (1 Corinthians 4:15-16).

How bold for Paul to say such things. Follow me as I follow God. Yet, this is what Jesus Christ did. He followed God the Father fully as he invited 12 others to experience life with him. They, in turn, imitated him.

Likewise, God has placed disciples in our homes. We may not have 12, but however many children God gives us, the principle is the same. We must imitate Jesus so our children will imitate us.

I'm a crummy example, you may reason. We all are. All mothers fail. All mothers raise their voices. All mothers live with regret. I've found comfort, however, in Hebrews 13:7-8: "Remember your leaders, who spoke the word of God to you. Consider the outcome of their way of life and imitate their faith. Jesus Christ is the same yesterday and today and forever."

We are the leaders who speak the Word of God to our children. We must consider our way of life so that our faith is something our children want to imitate. We must live in such a way that we wouldn't be ashamed of the manner in which our children copycat us. What I love about the Hebrews passage is the juxtaposition of verses 7 and 8—we are examples, yet Jesus is the same.

The joy is this: I may fail, but Jesus Christ is the same perfect Savior. He is the same in the past, covering over and forgiving my parenting sins. He is the same in the present, giving me strength to comfort a hurting child. He is the same in the future, enabling me to face an empty nest with resilience. He is the same. He is the One who helps me parent. He is the One I must point to.

As Paul pastored churches, he pointed his flock to Christ. He welcomed their imitation, but only because he was following Jesus. "Follow my example, as I follow the example of Christ" (1 Corinthians 11:1).

As mothers, we must follow Jesus—in his steps. But even more than that, we must live our lives in such a way that our children recognize that it's Jesus within us doing the work. We don't merely want to follow Jesus for our own recognition, to merely be copycatted for our own reward. Jesus said, "Let your light shine before men, that they may see your good deeds and *praise your Father in heaven*" (Matthew 5:16, emphasis mine).

The next time I ask Julia what she wants to be when she grows up, I hope she'll say something like, "I want to be a mommy who shows her children Jesus."

I'm being watched, Lord. In light of that, enable me to live in such a way that I honor you, point to you, and give you the credit. Thank you that you never change—that you're the Lord of the past, present, and future. I want to imitate you today, Jesus, so that my children can imitate me.

23

EARN A STRESS
LESS BADGE

Clee

THE GIRL SCOUTS OF AMERICA launched a new merit badge—the Stress Less Badge. The circular badge, framed in Girl Scout green, sports a tree, a sun peeking through wispy clouds, and a gently swinging hammock.

As a parent, I see the toll stress takes on my children. Sophie takes standardized tests and frets. Aidan worries about a turncoat friend. Julia cowers in the presence of the mean lunch ladies in her new French school. Victimized by errand running (by a mom who has *not* earned her Stress Less Badge), all three children bicker.

Stress is like an insidious disease; it moves and lives to find victims. But more often than I would like to admit, it is a congenital disease, passed surreptitiously from parents to children. When I worry about finances, the kids seem on edge. When I am running late, Sophie takes on her adult tone and scolds the other two for meandering.

Now that Patrick and I know about the Stress Less Badge, I think it is our prerogative to earn it on behalf of our family. We live in an age of dwindling childhood, where kids carry pagers and cram Day-Timers full of sports, clubs, homework, and work. With all the rushing around, we have lost the concept of unstructured (non-media) playtime. We have lost much of the innocence of playing games, eating together around the dinner table, and looking at the stars.

What are some real solutions? Following are three that just might earn the Girl Scout seal of approval.

Slow down. Gandhi said that there was more to life than increasing its speed. Somehow we have bought into the notion that cramming our days will mean a higher quality of life. For me, when I have come to the end of a hectic day, I am drained. When I am drained, pleas from my children to play with them fall on deaf ears. Even this week, Sophie said, "I wish you wouldn't pay the bills so much. I want to play with you." We mock cultures that have slower paces, calling them lazy or unproductive. But I wonder, how much real life has passed me by in my race for productivity? How many times have I glossed over an accomplishment of my child because my mind is tortuously cluttered with to-do lists? Instead, God tells us, "Be still, and know that I am God" (Psalm 46:10). When was the last time you were still?

Take a media break. Psychologist Mary Pipher, in her book *The Shelter of Each Other,* speaks of the damage of the media and its potential to add stress. She recounts an interesting story about a girl from Tonga. Pipher asked what it would be like to grow up in a world without media. The girl responded, "I never saw television...until I came to the United States in high school. I had a happy childhood. I felt safe all the time. I didn't know I was poor. Or that parents hurt their children or that children hated their parents. I thought I was pretty."[11] The only way to lessen the media's influence is to choose as a family to spend time together without its blaring intrusion. We need to set the example of quieting our souls. "I have stilled and quieted my soul; like a weaned child with its mother, like a weaned child is my soul within me" (Psalm 131:2). It's hard to quiet our souls or expect quiet souls in our children when there is so much noise cluttering our ears and so many flickering images clamoring for our attention.

Simplify. Henry David Thoreau noted, "Our life is frittered away by detail...Simplify, simplify, simplify!"[12] Growing up, I had a cluttered bedroom; as an adult, I have learned to de-clutter. The less I have in my home, the less I have to worry about. Although my children initially protest, I can hear their sighs of relief after we've de-cluttered together, bringing order to their little habitations. G.K. Chesterton said that there are two ways to be satisfied: One is to continue to get more and more stuff. The other is to desire less. Paul said contentment is a secret to be learned: "I have learned to be content whatever the circumstances. I know what it is to be in need, and I know what it is to have plenty. I have learned the secret of being content in any and every situation, whether well fed or hungry, whether living in plenty or in want. I can do everything through him who gives me strength" (Philippians 4:11-13). In addition to de-cluttering my home and learning contentment with what I have, I have also learned to de-clutter my heart. Holding grudges and covering up makes for a complicated life. To live simply is to forgive, let go, grant grace, and remember that people are more important than things.

Lord, I pray you would help me to slow down. I lay my calendar at your feet. Take out what you will. It's all yours. Remind me to turn off the media so I can be still and hear your tender voice. Teach me simplicity and contentment so I can foster those same traits in my children.

24

GIVING OUR
EYEBALLS

*D*URING A FAMILY DEVOTION TIME, my husband asked Sophie what the phrase "an eye for an eye" meant. She replied, "Doesn't that mean we share an eye with someone who needs it?"

As mothers, we embody my daughter's naïve and kind sentiment. We give every part of ourselves to our children. If one needed an eye, we'd share ours. If another needed our spleen, we'd likely cut it out and hand it over. We're used to kids needing every part of us.

During the breastfeeding phase of motherhood, I remember feeling that too much of me was doled out—my milk, my breast, my time. Still, I am thankful I had the opportunity to pour myself out for the sake of another because in that sacrifice I learned more about Jesus—his sacrifice mingled with joy.

What exactly does motherhood require?

Our hearts. As mothers we give the deepest parts of us to our children. Like Paul, we open wide our hearts, creating space for each child with which God blesses us. "We have spoken freely to you, Corinthians, and opened wide our hearts to you" (2 Corinthians 6:11).

Our lives. We daily lay our lives down in many ways—whether it be laying aside a dream, being interrupted, going without, or delaying a career. Our love for our children compels us to give the essence of our lives to them as a joyful gift. "We loved you so much that we were delighted to share with you not only the gospel of God but our lives as well, because you had become so dear to us" (1 Thessalonians 2:8).

Our desire to be served. Thankless tasks plague motherhood. Never does an unclean toilet clean itself, nor does it rise up and call us blessed when we swab it. Motherhood is a servant profession. Often it lacks glamour. Yet in doing seemingly insignificant tasks with joy, we identify with Jesus. We serve our children because we are following the example of Christ. "Whoever wants to become great among you must be your servant, and whoever wants to be first must be your slave—just as the Son of Man did not come to be served, but to serve, and to give his life as a ransom for many" (Matthew 20:26-28).

Our sleep. Midnight feedings, little fingers poking us after bad dreams, a croupy six-year-old—all these dig into our sleep. Our daily tasks deprive us of sleep. Even the Proverbs 31 woman lacks sleep: "She gets up while it is still dark; she provides food for her family" (Proverbs 31:15). As one who suffers from insomnia, I lament lost sleep. It puts me in an edgy mood and makes it easier for me to snap at my children. With sleeplessness, I've had to determine to lean on God's strength. Mine fails when I'm sleep-deprived.

Our spare time. I remember going to a scrap-booking class at a friend's home. At the time I had three small children under five. After I reveled in one page completed, I realized the tyranny of scrap-booking. My mind wandered. *If all my photos are imprisoned in acid-free pages and it takes three weeks to build an album of this caliber, it will take me three years to catch up—and then several months to maintain an acid-free collection.* I had to die to having protected photos because I didn't have spare time to preserve them. Motherhood is a sacrifice of time. Like the excellent wife in the book of Proverbs, seldom are we idle. "She watches over the affairs of her household and does not eat the bread of idleness" (Proverbs 31:27).

Our thoughts. When Sophie was halfway through third grade, we considered pulling her out of school. She was having severe relational struggles. You can imagine all the thought time I used up wondering about Sophie's heart and how we were going to help her through the year. Today I am wearing a plastic bead necklace my son Aidan made me. When I look at it, I think of him. Mothers think. They worry. They treasure thoughts about their children, to be savored for a later date. Like Jesus' mother, we think about our children. "Mary treasured up all these things and pondered them in her heart" (Luke 2:19).

Mothers give so many parts away it's a wonder we have anything left. Thankfully, we have a Savior who pours rivers of living water into us whenever we ask for a drink. He enables us to give our hearts, lives, desires to be served, sleep, spare time, and our thoughts first to him and then to our children.

Lord, I am tired. So much of me is given away that I feel depleted. Renew me. Pour rivers of living water into my heart so I can give back to my children. Give me a heart that is happy to serve them. Forgive me for failing to come to you when I'm weary. Here I am. Fill me up.

25

HEAVILY
EVER AFTER

JULIA TOLD A STORY to her dollies and ended it by saying, "And she lived heavily ever after." I'm guessing those Cinderella types didn't anticipate such an ending. From the fairy-tale gallery, they must have hurled "boos" to Julia's ending.

We all love happy endings. We all want a life that concludes, "And she lived happily ever after." Perhaps veiled by consumption of romance novels that purport such an ending, we are frustrated when life's inevitabilities come crashing into our dreams. Somehow we've become Christian Buddhists, believing the point of life is to be freed from pain.

Yet pain comes in many packages. Our children don't rise up and call us blessed; instead, they bicker and argue back. Our husband doesn't notice our new haircut; instead, he complains that dishes are still in the sink. Our medical tests don't come back normal; instead, they show cancerous tissue. Our parents don't approve of our choices; instead, they compare us to other siblings who are "doing it right." Nearly every day we live in a world of unmet expectations—where happily ever after becomes heavily ever after.

Expectations. We all have them. We all mourn them. Sometimes I throw my hands heavenward and want to shout "Enough already!" When too many expectations go unmet, I tend to sink back into pessimism—a sort of Eeyore on steroids. "Woe is me," I'll declare. "Nothing good ever happens. Life is just hard and unbearable."

When I'm in this state, I have forgotten that "happily ever after" *does* exist—just not here on earth. While living in this temporary place, inhabiting our temporary bodies, we will have trials. First Peter 4:12-13 tells us not to be surprised. "Dear friends, do not be surprised at the painful trial you are suffering, as though something strange were happening to you, but rejoice that you participate in the sufferings of Christ so that you may be overjoyed when his glory is revealed."

One day we will be trial-less. One day we will see the glory of Jesus. One day we will have no more tears. That's what faith is all about. We believe there is more to life than suffering. There is more to life than living heavily ever after. There is more to life than disobedient children, dishes that don't do themselves, worry over cancer, and disapproving in-laws. All these trials constitute life, but they do not constitute life forever.

To combat expectations going unmet, we simply need to readjust our expectations. If we expect everything to be peachy, we will be disappointed. If we let every trial surprise and bludgeon us, we will live defeated lives. Instead, we must lift our eyes to the great, unseen future, where Christ's glory reigns.

When trials mount, when happily ever after alludes you in the present, take heart. Someday it will be different. "He will wipe every tear from their eyes. There will be no more death or mourning or crying or pain, for the old order of things has passed away. He who was seated on the throne said, 'I am making everything new!'" (Revelation 21:4-5).

And in the present, when trials seem to mount, James tells us, "When all kinds of trials and temptations crowd into your lives, my brothers, don't resent them as intruders, but welcome them

as friends! Realize that they come to test your faith and to produce in you the quality of endurance" (James 1:2-3 PHILLIPS).

It's difficult to welcome trials and unmet expectations as
friends. I'd rather see them as enemies. Perhaps we need to readjust our thinking to believe that trials have something beautiful within them, something that helps us learn deeper qualities
of faith, hope, and love. William Shakespeare wrote, "Sweet are
the uses of adversity, which, like the toad, ugly and venomous,
wears yet a precious jewel in his head."[13]

Today we live in the heavily ever after. In the midst of today's
trials, God will show us the jewel amid the toad. Someday we'll
live in the happily ever after. No matter where we are in our
journey—at the burgeoning of motherhood or on the brink of
an empty nest, we can be assured that God will walk the journey
with us, holding us when life crashes and whispering that the
happily ever after is just around the corner.

*Lord, I need your perspective of this life.
Trials mount. My expectations are shattered. Teach
me to live for the day when life will indeed be happily
ever after. Help me to welcome venomous toads as
friends, showing me the jewel within.*

26

LIFE IS SHORT

FEW DAYS BEFORE CHRISTMAS, a drunk driver hit us. We had been at Sophie's orchestra concert and were driving home a different route to "ooh" and "aah" over holiday lights. Patrick stopped at a red light when SLAM, we were hit from behind, forcing us all to play the unwitting role of crash dummies as we slid forward and back, our seatbelts blessedly taut. I was in the passenger seat, so I immediately got out and opened the sliding door of our van to check on our children. They, like me, were rattled, scared, and shaky, but they were okay.

I hugged them all in a fierce sort of motherly embrace, whispered soothing words, and rocked them gently while cars drove around the accident site. Patrick called the police. They told us to drive to another location. We waited in our van as the police evaluated the teetering driver.

When the driver tried to walk a straight line later for the police, we had to explain to our inquisitive children why the police were making him do it.

"Why is he walking funny, Mommy?" Sophie asked.

"We think he is drunk—that he had too much alcohol to drink," I replied, trying to sound matter-of-fact, quelling the shivers and shakes that tried to invade my voice.

Sophie hugged herself, trying to soothe her own shivers. "Can we pray? I think we need to pray. I am scared." We prayed—a thankful sort of prayer, the kind of guttural prayer that has few words but thousands of emotions. We were safe. We were alive.

Julia, the realist, and one who seems to be interested in swift and just judgment said, "Is he going to jail, Daddy?"

Patrick replied, "Yes, I think so, for three days."

"Not forever?"

"No, Julia, not forever."

After the driver was handcuffed, a police officer came over to our waiting van and asked us the names and ages of our children. Just the question made me shudder and revel—shudder that they could have been taken from me in a blink of a drunken eye, and revel that they now lived and breathed.

He asked that I come down to the station in 20 minutes to file a report—which I did. I sat in the waiting area for a few moments in awkward silence with the man's wife or girlfriend. She did not look up to catch my eye, and I felt an odd sort of sadness just looking at her. I was then called to the counter, and while the officer filled out paperwork, the sad woman left the precinct. I wondered if I would ever see her again, but even as I left the station, I walked by her in the night air. She stood fixed to the sidewalk, moving her gaze from her feet to the star-pocked sky. As I pulled away, my headlights brushed by her face. I felt sad again and said a prayer for her.

Life is short. We say that in casual conversations, half thinking we know what we are saying. Sometimes it takes a swift hit from behind to bring the essence of life into perspective. People matter. Life matters. Breathing is a gift. God gives breath to all of us—to an intoxicated driver who spends Christmas in jail, to a sad-faced woman who looks at the sky for answers, to my shaken children who will remember the day for the rest of their lives, to my husband and I who breathe unutterable thanks.

As I consider life's brevity, I'm reminded of several Scriptures:

Why, you do not even know what will happen tomorrow. What is your life? You are a mist that appears for a little while and then vanishes (James 4:14).

All men are like grass, and all their glory is like the flowers of the field (Isaiah 40:6).

Show me, O Lord, my life's end and the number of my days; let me know how fleeting is my life. You have made my days a mere handbreadth; the span of my years is as nothing before you. Each man's life is but a breath (Psalm 39:4-5).

Man is like a breath; his days are like a fleeting shadow (Psalm 144:4).

Be very careful, then, how you live—not as unwise but as wise, making the most of every opportunity, because the days are evil (Ephesians 5:15-16).

I hope we are never hit again by a drunk driver. Yet in that hope I pray I won't forget the lesson God taught us all. Life is a vapor. We're only here for a short time. May it be that today we live as if it were our last—lavishing love on our children, rejoicing in the moment, taking every opportunity to share Jesus with others, seeking to bring God glory every second.

Teach me to number my days, Lord. I want to live life with the understanding that it is fleeting. With eyes bent on the eternal, show me opportunities today to cherish my family and bless the people you bring in my path.

27

MOTHERHOOD FROM THE INSIDE OUT

*M*Y SON IS NOT FASHION CONSCIOUS; in fact, I'd rather consider him fashion unconscious. If left to himself, Aidan would walk out the door with backwards pants and inside-out shirts. Once, when Patrick got the kids ready for school one morning, I realized perhaps this was a genetic trait because when Aidan came home, he was inside out.

Motherhood is an inside-out endeavor. It's not merely that we perform outward duties—establishing an orderly home, falling into a weekly rhythm, disciplining when our children need it—it's that our hearts are engaged with our children. Given an outside-in look, I appear to have my motherhood all together (well, not always, but some days!). But if someone were to make an inside-out glance, they might find a disengaged heart.

My husband told me a story one day. In it, I was pacing back and forth on a high dive while he and the children beckoned me from a swimming pool far below. Arms crossed over my chest with a nervous look, I kept pacing.

They shouted, "Come on in! Dive in! The water's great!"

I peered over the edge of the board. I saw their laughter-infused antics, but I turned from them and walked to the other end of the board, eventually backing down the ladder. In Patrick's story, I walked tentative steps to the pool's edge and settled for putting my toe in the water while the rest of my family splashed and laughed and sang.

I long to be the spontaneous one who dives into the lives of my family, but I have disconnected somehow. I'm pretty good about the outside-in tasks of motherhood, but I find it difficult to connect with my children from my heart.

This is something all mothers need to explore. I realized that I had numbed myself from feeling as a result of a difficult childhood. My coping mechanism was to simply not let anyone into my heart because if I did, it would be shredded. Although I knew my little family and my dear husband were safe people, my fear prevented me from engagement. This self-imposed emotional anesthesia left me unconscious from the vitality of life; it prevented me from letting those I loved the most—especially my husband—into the recesses of my heart.

The journey from outside-in to inside-out is one I am walking today. It is a constant battle to stop my tasks of motherhood and enter into the pain of my children. When Sophie comes home complaining of a terrible day, my first instinct is to rationalize her pain away. With God's strength—and with too much failure to calculate—I am learning to stop what I am doing to ask her questions, to engage in her pain and feel it alongside her.

Like my friend Diane who grew up in a horrendous home—at times not having food to eat—all I can do is the ultimate inside-out task: pray. It's the invisible thing we do as parents, but it is perhaps the most important. As a parent with no frame of reference to go from and a heart that was shattered from her upbringing, Diane was bewildered. Still, she prayed. Her children have grown up to love Jesus, something that amazes her.

She told me, "The best thing I did in parenting them was to pray. I made a lot of mistakes, but I prayed."

So, I've prayed.

And I've had to humble myself before my children. I've had to apologize when I've not connected with them from the inside-out. I've asked them to pray for me. I've asked others to pray the Lord would heal more of my past so I could engage fully in the present.

I've lamented my inabilities. I've cried. I've asked the Lord to give me the courage to mount the high dive's rickety steps, to venture to the end of the board and swan dive into the hearts of my family. My prayers echo King David's: "What you're after is truth from the inside out. Enter me, then; conceive a new, true life...God make a fresh start in me, shape a Genesis week from the chaos of my life" (Psalm 51:6,10 MSG).

Jesus, I want to dive into the hearts of my family, but I'm pacing the high dive. Show me where I've failed to love them from the inside out, Lord. I want to dive in fully—both to their hearts and your arms.

28

No Presents,
Just Presence

Julia was recently invited to a birthday hoedown. The invitation read, "No presents, just your presence." Julia scribbled a card and we were off to the country to celebrate her friend Neeley with our presence. Not only were we thankful for the present moratorium, we also had a terrific time—bumping along in an old-fashioned hayride and torching once-white marshmallows.

I thought about how glued I can become to the presents of God and forget how amazing his presence is. His daily invitation to mothers is, "Seek me, not my stuff." Likewise, he asks of us, "Don't give me your stuff, just give me you."

Seek me, not my stuff. A friend told the story about her type A husband who left on a business trip. He had been expecting a certain bill to come in the mail while he was gone, so he called his wife several times a day asking if the bill had arrived yet. No "How are you?" or "How are the kids?"—only "Where's that bill?" This, of course, grated on her sensibilities. Instead of nagging—the sort of thing I'd do—she did something cleverly proactive. She sent the kids to a sitter so that when he came home, she'd be the only person there. When he opened the door, she stood in front of him bare naked, except for bills taped to her body. Her nonverbal encouragement screamed, "Seek me, not the stuff I do for you."

We were new to a church when a couple invited us for dinner. A bit lonely, we welcomed the invitation. However, when I put our coats in their bedroom, I noticed elaborate sales charts papering every wall. *Oh no,* I thought. *They're going to want us to "get in on the ground floor of this amazing opportunity."* After the evening, I told my husband about the charts.

"They wouldn't do that," he said. "They just wanted to have us over—to be kind."

Three days later we got the call. "We want you to get in on the ground floor of this amazing opportunity," the husband said. They wanted our presents (money and time), not our presence.

Similarly, God wants us to seek him not merely for the functions he performs but just for the sheer joy of relationship with him. He is concerned about the smallest trials of our lives, not so much so he can fix them (although he sometimes does), but so that he can hold our hand through them. His gifts of help and encouragement are icing on the cake, but he is the cake.

Don't give me your stuff, just give me you. The Bible is peppered with this truth: God is not as interested in our sacrifices as he is interested in our heart toward him. In Psalm 51:16-17, David said, "You do not delight in sacrifice, or I would bring it; you do not take pleasure in burnt offerings. The sacrifices of God are a broken spirit; a broken and contrite heart, O God, You will not despise." He wants our hearts, broken and empty, so he can fill them with himself. Hosea 6:6 admonishes, "For I desire mercy, not sacrifice, and acknowledgment of God rather than burnt offerings."

In the New Testament, one of the teachers of the Law defied his legalistic cronies by saying: "To love him [God] with all your heart, with all your understanding and with all your strength, and to love your neighbor as yourself is more important than all burnt offerings and sacrifices" (Mark 12:33). To this man who "got it" Jesus replied, "You are not far from the kingdom of God" (verse 34). Jesus wants all of us—not just an appearance of sacrifice, but also our very being. As mothers, we are to love Jesus and turn around and disseminate that love to our husband and children. That is God's desire.

The takeaway truth for mothers is this: It's not our sacrificial motherly performance he's after—it's our heart and how well we love him and others. It's not that we run well on the treadmill called home life, but that we dare to jump off and run toward him and the children he places in our care.

God invites us to his eternal hoedown, seeking our presence, not our presents. In like manner, we need to daily invite him to our family hoedown, requesting and relishing his presence in our family more than the presents he often gives. His presents may decorate our walls, but it's his presence that transforms the heart of our homes.

Heavenly Father, help me to seek your presence more than your presents. Spotlight where I've valued stuff over valuing my relationship with you. Show me today how I've held myself back from loving you and my children. I can't do this holy job called motherhood without you.

29

SPANKING PRACTICE

AIDAN ANNOUNCED ONE NIGHT at the dinner table, "I'm practicing to be a daddy. I've practiced by spanking myself. It sounds like it hurts but it doesn't."

It's interesting how my children view parenthood from their rib-high perspective. Aidan, obviously, thinks parenting involves mostly spanking, so he's practicing now—just in case.

On the other hand, Julia thinks parenting is all about acquiescing to a child's every whim. She told us, "I want a mommy and daddy who only say YES to Julia." She tells her dolls yes all the time while peeking out of the corner of her eye to see if we are watching. I think she wishes we would follow her example. It's a good thing for her that her dolls don't talk back. If they did, they'd show how utterly spoiled they'd become under her indulgent tutelage.

Sophie thinks parenthood is all about being completely fair at any given moment. After stamped feet she often says, "It's not faaaaiiiir" for all to hear. Maybe she hopes if she elongates the word *fair* and says it especially loud, we will instantly become the fairest parents on the block.

I used to view parenthood as my children did—one dimensionally. I thought it was a simple endeavor—like washing dishes or tying shoes. But parenthood is more than spanking or indulgence or fairness. It's about lifestyle. Parenthood is a balancing act between many teetering extremes. Strict or lenient. Carefree or structured. Protecting or granting freedom.

We come into parenting with a backpack full of great, untried ideas. Some of the ideas spring from what we observed as children. We want to emulate what our parents did well and eliminate what we view as their failures. We pull out each idea, nurse it, and place it back inside, smug and assured that when our offspring come along, we'll be the best parents God has ever entrusted with children.

Patrick and I had many wonderful ideas in that backpack, and we'd pull out our ideas when other parents seemed to be flailing. We'd watch little Joshua wreak holy terror, sigh, and look at each other with a knowing glance. We would never allow our progeny to become tyrannical like Joshua. Something was wrong with those parents! They needed to look in our backpack!

Then children came squealing into our lives. They instinctively knew about our backpack. Once Sophie crawled, she headed to the bulging backpack and unpacked it, splaying its contents over the family room. At once we were found out—by a small crawling human donning a saggy diaper. We realized that we too were inept, needy folks who didn't really know what we were doing.

Unveiled and backpack-less, we understood our absolute need for God. We underlined home-metaphor verses like "Unless the LORD builds the house, its builders labor in vain. Unless the LORD watches over the city, the watchmen stand guard in vain" (Psalm 127:1) and "Therefore everyone who hears these words of mine and puts them into practice is like a wise man who built his house on the rock. The rain came down, the streams rose, and the winds blew and beat against the house; yet it did not fall, because it had its foundation on the rock" (Matthew 7:24-25).

We realized that our parenting was not a simple formula of our own devising. It needed to be linked to the Lord. We knew that to love our children with the winsome love of the heavenly Father, we had to be deeply connected with him ourselves. The truth is, in our own strength, our homes will tumble when the storms of life crash in. We cannot build a family strong enough in our own feeble strength.

Perhaps that's why my favorite verse encourages me so much. I am a weak mother. I yell when I shouldn't. I cry in exasperation when I should run to Jesus for strength. I fail to spend deep, abiding time with my children. I agonize over my shortcomings. But Jesus whispers to me amid my failures: "My grace is sufficient for you, for my power is made perfect in weakness" (2 Corinthians 12:9).

So, maybe it's not that I do everything perfectly, but it's that I recognize my dire need for Jesus. I love Paul's response to Jesus' statement about his power perfected in weakness. Paul declares, "Therefore I will boast all the more gladly about my weaknesses, so that Christ's power may rest on me. That is why, for Christ's sake, I delight in weaknesses, in insults, in hardships, in persecutions, in difficulties. For when I am weak, then I am strong" (2 Corinthians 12:9-10).

There is comfort in understanding I don't have to know everything there is to know about parenting. All I can do is acknowledge and delight in my weakness so the Lord can build my home upon his rock.

I thought I had all the parenting answers, Lord, but I now understand I don't. What does it mean to delight in my weakness? Show me. I need your strength. I need your strong arm. Parent my children through me today. Build our family upon your rock today.

30

GRIEF AND THE IDOL
OF SELF-PROTECTION

When I attended Aidan's first grade author's night,
I didn't realize I'd learn about death, life, and grief—or that God
would use the words of children to show me my propensity to
hide from life.

Earlier that day Aidan came home and said a cryptic,
"Mommy, I can't tell you who I dedicated my book to. It's a
secret." Then he blushed, ate a snack, and did his homework.
That evening we sat hunched forward, trying to hear small
voices echo above the cacophony of two other squirrelly classes
in the cafeteria.

More than one book was about a well-loved pet—something
to the effect of "Spotty liked to eat. Spotty licked my face. Spotty
was very cute."

Was? *Oh no,* I thought. *This is not going to end well.*

"Spotty went to the vet and never came home. He died. I
cried."

One by one, we became privy to the private doom of a crab
and several dogs. I thought about what this might mean in the
grand scheme of things. I've come to the conclusion that adults

mourn in a backward sort of way and we could learn a thing or two from these grieving first graders.

We use the words "passed away" or "loss," while children use "death." We try to pretend we are going to be fine when a pet or friend or relative dies, while children cry. We try to deny the reality of death—that if we don't speak of it, it won't reach its icy grip into our homes, while children acknowledge its existence and finality.

You know what? I want to cry when I am sad. I want to say the simple truth. Death hurts. Death is final. Death makes me cry. Death is never easy to get over. Death is the loss of a relationship. Because God created us for relationships, death agonizes me. It makes me lonely. I remember that oft-memorized verse, "Jesus wept" (John 11:35) and comfort myself that even Jesus shed tears when he lost a friend.

After the stinging loneliness of death, the children served me another lesson—the lesson of moving on. They mourned Crabby's loss and looked forward to new Crabbies and new Spotties. They had a wide-eyed expectancy of what was to come.

Some of us die when death hits close to us. That's it. No moving on, no more relational investment, no more risk, no more deep happiness. We numb ourselves to the tragedies of life as well as its joys. We live somewhere in the world of mediocre sameness, moving throughout our days in a haze of surface living.

Perhaps that's why we live in a medicated society. Unlike the children in Aidan's class, we don't cry, or if we do, we do it alone behind closed doors. Eventually our hearts close. We deadbolt our emotions, deeming them unacceptable. If a circumstance threatens to unlock our deadbolt, we medicate, further numbing ourselves from life's pain.

I have lived that way before. It's called a life half-lived. Sure, I am insulated from the pain, but I am also cut off from the deepest joys. You can't have joy without its twin: pain. You can't have wholehearted belly laughter without gut-heaving sobs.

Scotty Smith in his book entitled *Speechless* has harsh words for those living half-lived lives: "In my commitment never to hurt again, I basically chose to worship an idol—self-protection."[14] If I look at my life—really peel away the layers—I shudder to think of how much of it is lived worshiping the idol of self-protection. I wonder how much energy I expend protecting my heart from pain and displeasure. And I wonder how that has stifled my relationship with the weeping Savior.

Watch children. Watch them live. They cry and get over it. Then they play. Someone makes a face and they laugh. They live life as it should be lived—in the actual moment. Oh, to live in the moment, instead of groveling over the past, fretting about the present, or speculating on future doom. Oh, to live life today, emotions and all. Maybe that's why Jesus told us to welcome and become like children. "Let the little children come to me, and do not hinder them, for the kingdom of God belongs to such as these. I tell you the truth, anyone who will not receive the kingdom of God like a little child will never enter it" (Luke 18:16-17).

I lived in the moment on author's night. One book stood out above the others. I thought to myself, *Wow, that's a beautifully illustrated book.* I smiled when Aidan picked up that very book, opened it, and read, "This book is dedicated to my mommy." I am sure he read other words, but I could hear only those.

Lord, make me like a child again—trusting, grieving, laughing. I don't want to worship the idol of self-protection. I want to engage life, to weep at its maladies, and laugh at its hilarities. Show me where I'm disengaged.

31

THRESHING FLOOR
OFFERINGS

WHEN OUR ELDEST DAUGHTER Sophie turned eleven, I asked family members and adult friends to send her birthday cards with growing up advice. Because she was born on Christmas Eve, people often overlooked her special day. Imagine her delight when we handed her cards and letters from all over America the morning of her birthday.

In the stack was a letter from me.

Sophie was struggling with our decision to move from Texas to become church planters in France. She was afraid she'd look stupid, not knowing French. She cried about leaving her friends behind. She worried she'd have a hard time making friends. She wished we could move back to Seattle, our home. When acquaintances asked her what she thought about moving, she shrugged and walked away. This, of course, broke my heart. I'd lament, *What kind of mother am I that I would take my child away from everything familiar to a place where I know she'll be mocked and ridiculed for her faith?* We'd received upsetting emails from team members already on the field detailing how their eldest (Sophie's age) was getting tripped by bullies at school.

I wrestled with Sophie's grief. I agonized. I remembered Oswald Chambers' words: "If we obey God, it is going to cost other people more than it costs us, and that is where the sting comes in…We can disobey God if we choose, and it will bring immediate relief to the situation, but we shall be a grief to our Lord. Whereas if we obey God, he will look after those who have been pressed into the consequences of our obedience. We have simply to obey and to leave all consequences with him."[15]

I wanted to please Jesus more than anything, and now with Sophie's sadness, I was counting the cost in ways I never imagined. My obedience was costing Sophie—her comfort, her possible persecution, her sense of home. With that as a backdrop, I tucked this note among the others she received on her birthday.

> *On this, your eleventh birthday, I want to encourage you to walk in King David's shoes. He wanted to erect an altar to the Lord and worship him. He approached a man about some land. He wanted to buy it to make the altar there, but the man, Araunah, said David could have the land for free. David responded this way: "No, but I will surely buy it from you for a price, for I will not offer burnt offerings to the LORD my God which cost me nothing" (2 Samuel 24:24 NASB).*
>
> *Sophie, this year as we move away from everything comfortable, you have the unique opportunity to offer something to God that costs you everything. Sacrifice is hard. David could have easily taken the land for free and then offered his sacrifices to God, but then they wouldn't be difficult.*
>
> *Sometimes God asks us to do hard things for the sake of his kingdom. You now have a choice—to understand that life is a series of humbling circumstances. We may not always love where God takes us, and we may not like it or understand his ways, but eventually, I pray you'll understand what a privilege it is he's given you to offer your whole self to him, no matter how hard it is or at what cost.*

"Therefore I urge you, [Sophie], by the mercies of God, to present your [body] as a living and holy sacrifice, acceptable to God, which is your spiritual service of worship" (Romans 12:1 NASB). May it be that as you grow into a beautiful, sweet, righteous, happy, contented woman, you understand what a joy it is to follow Jesus, and how very deeply he loves you and longs to carry you through every difficulty you face.

As mothers we don't want to see our children suffer. We'd do anything to prevent it. But, through this time of pain, I've been able to see God meet Sophie where she is. We've had hundreds of people pray for her. We've had the joy of watching her change from begrudging our move to France to saying, "I am looking forward to it."

Sometimes our obedience to Christ costs our children. But God is always big enough to walk in the midst of their pain, holding them tighter than we can, and maturing them in ways we couldn't.

Jesus, I want to follow you wherever you lead. I want to have a willing heart to do whatever it is you have called me to, even if it costs my children. Help me to understand that you love them infinitely more than I can. Help me to step into your plan with joy, knowing that you hold my family in the palm of your hand.

32

LESSONS AROUND
THE DINING TABLE

Cee

FOOD. IT CAN BE a four-letter word in our family—especially for Aidan, who has mastered the art of portion pushing. While rabid when eating anything breadlike (does the fact that we call him "dough-boy" give you an indication of his deep affection for anything carbohydrate?), he becomes achingly slow eating green or meatlike items.

Recently we had sweet-and-sour fish stir-fry—not one of his favorite meals. After shoveling several bucketfuls of white rice down his gullet, he pulled a tiny sinew off a piece of fish and said, "I can't swallow it. It gets stuck in my throat."

Like Aidan, we get stuck in a spiritual food rut. We run to the Psalms in a pinch, neglecting Ecclesiastes and Nahum. We content ourselves to pray hurried words before meals, calling that our prayer life. We do what is familiar, routine. We prefer that which is easy. Yet God often calls us away from familiarity. He beckons us to the margins where stir-fried fish and the unfamiliar live.

Contrast Aidan's single-hearted devotion to bread with Sophie, who loves salad and artichokes and asparagus. She tries everything and usually likes everything. When Aidan came along, I just didn't know what to do. I was spoiled by Sophie's eclectic palate. I had to remind myself that I, too, was a picky eater. It helps me have grace.

There's a spiritual lesson for mothers here. If we always run to the latest and greatest treats of spiritual life while neglecting the staples, we'll flounder. Jesus declared, "I am the bread of life. He who comes to me will never go hungry, and he who believes in me will never be thirsty" (John 6:35). Like Aidan, we must eat our daily Bread—in the form of communing with Jesus all day long.

Julia's food affinity is for anything smacking of condiments. A complete meal for her would be one (or two!) pickles, a quarter cup ketchup, and three tablespoons mustard. She is just now venturing into the phenomenon called ranch dressing. Today I coined a new physiological term for her...she has condimental illness.

We all need condimental illness—we need to become salt to a tasteless world. Jesus said, "You are the salt of the earth. But if the salt loses its saltiness, how can it be made salty again? It is no longer good for anything, except to be thrown out and trampled by men" (Matthew 5:13). In neighborhoods where marriages are fizzling and children are rebelling, we are salt. We season our spheres of influence with the life of Jesus Christ.

One thing that has had an effect on our overall family diet is Patrick's recent cholesterol screening. Let's just say he didn't get an A. Gone are the nights when he settled down to a man-sized bowl of cholesterol cleverly disguised as Ben and Jerry's. Now he grimaces at ice milk products made by Healthy Choice. No more two percent milk either—it's the blue stuff for him.

Julia has taken up a crusade against cholesterol. In her four-year-old mind, cholesterol is some malevolent force that kills people. Every time we sit down to eat, she asks, "Daddy, does that have cholesterol in it?" She looks relieved when he says no. Last week she played with her dollhouse. She carried the plastic mommy to the roof and flung her off so that she landed face down on the patio below. Julia made the little plastic daughter rush to her immediate aid (as all good plastic daughters should do when their mommy is flung off roofs by giant blonde girls). The daughter said, in Julia's impish voice, "Are you okay? Did you eat too much cholesterol?"

With the vigilance of Julia, we need to crusade against the one who "comes to steal, kill and destroy" (John 10:10). Like cholesterol, the devil is a stealthy killer, stalking us unaware and poisoning our hearts. Peter encourages us to "be self-controlled and alert. Your enemy the devil prowls around like a roaring lion looking for someone to devour" (1 Peter 5:8).

Open my eyes to your lessons, Lord, even the lessons you have for me around the dinner table tonight. Help me to follow you wherever you lead me, even in the unfamiliar. I want to eat your Bread of Life. I want to be your salt to a tasteless world. Show me today where Satan is prowling.

33

CONFIDENCE
FROM JESUS

My HEART HAS CONDEMNED ME.

Haunted by images of my motherly failures, I have made it a habit to berate myself for my lack of parenting ability—and with good reason. I grew up in a home I did not want to duplicate. I did not want my children to experience the childhood I lived. So, every mistake I made, I worried that I was reproducing a painful childhood for them. The fear felt like a wet blanket over my body—heavy, cold, and suffocating.

The insecurity I've felt about creating a good home is at times a casual fear, at others a noose fixing itself around my neck. Yet in the midst of this God used two incidents to revive my heart and slice away at my parental fears.

In the summer of 1999, my friend Heidi flew from Idaho to visit our family in East Texas. She needed a break from routine, and God knew I needed Heidi's words. We spent the week together taking the kids to the zoo, visiting local sites, and just hanging out. We ate ribs at the Rib Shack—a restaurant whose slogan is "the best ribs you ever did eat." We laughed. We talked late into the evenings and we prayed together.

At the end of her stay, she held my gaze. "You're a good mother, Mary. Your children know you love them." Her words were a gift I'll never forget. I have feared for so long that my children wouldn't know I loved them because in my upbringing, I wasn't sure if my mother loved me. So much of my childhood was spent feeling in the way that I had a titanic fear I would project that same feeling onto my children. To realize a friend saw that my children knew I loved them eased much of my worry.

Two years after hearing Heidi's words, I sat on the loveseat in our Texas living room reading my Bible. It was 9:30 in the evening. I remember the time because at the moment I heard God's voice echo in my head, I looked up at the wall clock. Softly, the Lord said, "Mary, I want you to say you are a good mother. Out loud."

"Really?"

"Yes. Say it."

I pulled my knees to my chest, wrapping my arms around myself. I took a deep breath and said, "I am a good mother." As soon as the words left my mouth, a weight, leaden and dark, lifted from me. In those spoken words, I tasted freedom for the first time in nine years of parenthood. The Lord wanted me to declare his ability out loud, to shout it to the rooftops, that I was a good mother, not because of my own inherent goodness, but because of his obvious healing of my wounded childhood.

The only way I could say those five difficult words was because the God of the universe saw fit to pluck me out of my circumstances and heal my needy heart. He's in the habit of taking hurting mothers and transforming them into dependent ones. Consider how The Message renders 1 Corinthians 1:27-30: "Isn't it obvious God deliberately chose men and women that the culture overlooks and exploits and abuses, chose these 'nobodies' to expose the hollow pretensions of the 'somebodies'? That makes it quite clear that none of you can get by with blowing your own horn before God. Everything that we have—

right thinking and right living, a clean slate and a fresh start—comes from God by way of Jesus Christ."

All mothers fail. All are haunted. If I were to poll the readers of this book, I'd see that a great majority of us have hearts that condemn us. Many of us live under a cloud of guilt for our failures as mothers. Some of us worry that our adult children will end up in counseling—and that we will be the reason for their emotional distress. Perhaps today is the day you need to declare, through the power of the Holy Spirit who lives within you, that you are a good mother.

Remember, the condemning voice does not belong to Jesus. His is the cheerleader voice. He lifts us when we fail, dusts us off, and places us on a new path. He longs for us to have confidence before him. Consider this: "This then is how we know that we belong to the truth, and how we set our hearts at rest in his presence whenever our hearts condemn us. For God is greater than our hearts, and he knows everything. Dear friends, if our hearts do not condemn us, we have confidence before God" (1 John 3:19-21).

The command in those verses is that we "set our hearts at rest" whenever guilt and fear creep in. Today, determine to set your heart at rest, knowing that he will not condemn. His promise to mothers is that he "gently leads those that have young" (Isaiah 40:11).

I need your gentle leadership, Jesus. I live in fear and guilt and shame. Enable me to declare I am a good mother. Help me to realize you choose the weak to show your strength. I give you my children and the outcome of my parenting. I love you, Jesus.

34

TENT WHINING

I LOVE THE DEFINITION OF "WHINE": a complaining, long-drawn wail as of a dog, a similar shrill, prolonged sound. My five-year-old is a master at whining. After a while all Julia's words morph together into one incessant dog wail, and I have to walk away, anxious for a whine break.

Of course, I annoy my children—who have suffered from varying degrees of whine illness—by saying, "I can't hear you when you whine. Please speak in a normal voice."

As grating as whining can be to my ears, I wonder how my own whining sounds to God's ears. I've been guilty of wailing my prayers, of only considering my own pain. Consider how the psalmist renders our whining: "They soon forgot what he had done and did not wait for his counsel…They forgot the God who saved them, who had done great things in Egypt…They grumbled in their tents and did not obey the LORD" (Psalm 106:13,21,25).

Grumbled in their tents—an interesting metaphor. The Israelites had seen the amazing power of God. Through Moses, he sent frogs and made rivers bloody. He divided the Red Sea and licked its ground dry. He let the waters fold over the

Egyptian army, not sparing one. He provided food out of nothing—every day feeding the Israelites with heavenly bread smacking of honey. For 40 years he did not allow their sandals to wear out. He brought them water and meat. And yet in their tents they grumbled.

Mothers, in the midst of grumbling children (and sometimes husbands!), grumble too. We follow in the Israelite's sandaled footsteps.

We forget. In one 24-hour period, our pilot light went out, we didn't get a crucial scholarship, we received an unexpected bill in the mail, my first-ever mammogram was abnormal, a creepy guy approached me after a writing presentation I gave, and my husband left on a business trip for ten days while my children were on spring break. What did I do? I panicked. I forgot to trace the hand of God through my past. He had been utterly faithful to me, yet I had forgotten. Trials, when they smack us in the face, can make us forget.

We do not wait for his counsel. How quickly I run to panic and whining instead of stopping and listening for his voice. Often I don't take the time needed to quiet myself, to hear his encouragement.

We grumble. Many of us live complaint-based lives. I used to soften my pessimism by calling it realism. Truth be told, I am a pessimist. When things happen—bad or good—I automatically assume the worst will befall me, and then I whine. Yet God calls us all to praise him whether our forecast is cheerful or dismal. When whining overtakes us, we need to become like Habakkuk: "Though the fig tree does not bud and there are no grapes on the vines, though the olive crop fails and the fields produce no food, though there are no sheep in the pen and no cattle in the stalls, yet I will rejoice in the LORD, I will be joyful in God my Savior" (Habakkuk 3:17-18).

We disobey the Lord in our whining. We forget that forgetting what God has done and living a complaint-based life is called disobedience. Put simply, incessant whining is a sin. Yes, we should pray, but we should pour out our hearts before him *as* we remember what he's done and praise him in the midst of our current deprivation.

I'm afraid mothers and children alike are tent whiners. Paul equates our bodies with tents. "Now we know that if the earthly tent we live in is destroyed, we have a building from God, an eternal house in heaven, not built by human hands" (2 Corinthians 5:1). While we walk this earth in our body-tents, be assured that there will be mishaps and struggles that make us want to whine. Next time you are tempted to forget the mighty hand of God, listen to your children's whining and endeavor to lift praise to the heavens rather than a complaint. That praise will be music to the Lord's ears.

Lord, I am a tent whiner. I forget what you have done. I don't stop and listen for your still, quiet voice. I jump to pessimism, worrying that the worst will befall me. Forgive me for not praising you through my trials, Lord. Even if the fig tree doesn't bud today, I want to praise you anyway.

35

THE SISTERHOOD
OF MOTHERHOOD

You MAY NOT CONSIDER YOURSELF a baboon, but an interesting study in the journal *Science* has some compelling implications for today's mothers.[16] The study analyzed 108 female baboons and their mothering habits in Kenya. It revealed that baboon mothers who had a network of female friends were more successful in their mothering than their poor friendless counterparts.

Perhaps it is because baboons within social circles, similar to old-time quilting bees and new-fangled online affinity groups, can pick the bugs out of each other's fur. I'd like to think that friendship-welcoming women and baboons alike are just plain nicer when they have been picked clean and have a place to vent or growl their frustrations.

What happens, though, if you currently struggle with your friendships? What if you lack friends? What can you do to create or cultivate a sisterhood of motherhood? The secret lies within an unlikely friendship between two men, David and Jonathan. "David...bowed down before Jonathan three times, with his face to the ground. Then they kissed each other and wept together— but David wept the most" (1 Samuel 20:41).

Be humble. David bowed before his friend with his face to the ground. He did not elevate himself or disdain his need for a friend. Instead, he honored him. Being humble is the opposite of being prideful. To attract and keep friends, we must be willing to serve. We must be willing to bend the knee and consider the friend as more important than ourselves. We must be willing to admit our failures and ask humbly for forgiveness. Be a humble friend, and you will endear yourself to other mothers.

Be affectionate. David kissed Jonathan—a very tender act showing the depth of their intimacy. Touch your friends when you pray. Hug with your words and deeds—send emails, call, write cards, offer to take care of someone's children. Part of affection is loving others the way they truly experience love. Find out how a friend or future friend likes to be loved and choose to love her that way. Proverbs 17:17 tells us how often we should endeavor to love this way: "A friend loves at all times."

Weep and laugh. One of the hallmark Scriptures of friendship is, "Rejoice with those who rejoice; mourn with those who mourn" (Romans 12:15). When a friend is sorrowful, weep. When a friend rejoices, don't begrudge, but rejoice with her. The truest mark of a friendship is whether you can rejoice with a friend.

Be vulnerable. To invite someone into your world of motherhood, you have to be willing to let down your mask, to invite friends over to a cluttered home. Consider the deep vulnerability of David with his friend Jonathan. He let Jonathan see him at his weakest. To cultivate friendships, we must be willing to do the same.

I'm not one to believe I'm kin to primates, but in this case, I think scientists are on to something. I am a better mother when I have made a concerted effort to develop my friendships.

We are not a village raising children—that's the parent's job—but within a community of sisterhood, we can shoulder each other's burdens simply because we wear the same burdens every day and know where they chafe.

We can vent our stress to our friends, deflecting our anger away from our children and processing it before we talk to our little people. We can say, "I understand," and weep as we realize the weight of motherhood's task. A sisterhood of mothers sanitizes us and brings a hilarious sanity to the world's hardest profession.

So, the baboons are on to something. In community, they mother better. Next time your mommy-frustration levels hit the ceiling, call a baboon, er, a friend. Be careful, though—she might just pick the bugs out of your hair!

Dear Jesus, I need your help. Please send me other mothers who are humble, will love me for who I am, will weep and laugh with me, and will welcome authenticity and vulnerability. Forgive me for not being a good friend. Forgive me for trying to be a Lone Ranger mommy. Surround me afresh with the friends you have planned for me so that I can love my children and husband more fully.

36

THE LAMENT PSALM
OF MOTHERHOOD

REMEMBER THE PLAYGROUND of your childhood? Set right in the middle of wood chips was the seesaw, a wonderful contraption if you happened to have a benevolent soul on the other end. If, however, you had a short scrappy kid named Andre on the other end, a bruised tailbone awaited you.

I was thinking about seesaws today as our teaching pastor worked through a lament psalm. True to form, Psalm 13 follows a typical lament format. It begins with David's sadness—a questioning of whether God sees him: "How long, O LORD? Will you forget me forever? How long will you hide your face from me? How long must I wrestle with my thoughts and every day have sorrow in my heart? How long will my enemy triumph over me?" (verses 1-2).

Although our children can't be classified as enemies, there have been times of motherhood when I've felt God hide his face. There have been moments of motherhood where I've wrestled with nagging thoughts, particularly whether I am damaging my children with my impatience or lack of face-to-face attention. I've sorrowed over my children's sorrows. Like David, I've lamented.

The second part of the psalm is a prayer to God, a petition for his provision: "Look on me and answer, O LORD my God. Give light to my eyes, or I will sleep in death; my enemy will say, 'I have overcome him,' and my foes will rejoice when I fall" (verses 3-4).

I have breathed similar prayers as I've folded laundry. I've asked God to give light to my eyes as I've stumbled through midnight feedings. I've pleaded for God's distant voice to thunder back to me in restorative reply.

The last part of this lament psalm is a hymn of praise: "But I trust in your unfailing love; my heart rejoices in your salvation. I will sing to the LORD, for he has been good to me" (verses 5-6).

Something has happened after the petition. God has heard the lamenter's prayer, rejuvenating David's weary heart with new faith. I've breathed this praise when God met me during a particularly impatient day. Not of my own merit, my praise to God was a testimony of his capacity to encourage me, a fainthearted mother.

As I meditate on this, I realize a lament psalm is like a seesaw. As mothers, we tend to sway on either end. My tendency is to camp on the lament side, woe-is-me-ing my way through life. Others Polly-Anna through life, camping on the praise side and possibly ignoring the lessons life's deeper pains produce.

Neither is healthy. The fulcrum of our lives must pivot on the middle part of the lament—the petition.

If I am always lamenting, never whispering hymns of praise in the darkness, I'll despair. My way out is to pray—to ask the God of the universe to help me in my parenthood, in my wifehood, in my friendhood. Only after praying, only after meeting Jesus in the darkness, can I sing his praises.

If I am always praising and never delving into the lessons he wants to teach me in the darkness, my way out is still to pray. I can ask the God of light to shed his candle on the darker parts of my heart. I can ask him to teach me to walk David's path of lament, from one pool of light to the next, one step at a time.

The seesaw psalm rests on the fulcrum of prayer—of finite humanity reaching for an infinite Savior. If we tend toward sadness, he will turn our lament into praise. If we tend toward living on the surface of life, he will pull us deeper.

The joy of the whole analogy is that Jesus keeps us in balance if we look first to him. The up and down of seesaw living ceases as we pour our hearts out to him. Lamenting and praising both become the tenets of our lives if he is our fulcrum.

Lord, help me to ask for your help when I'm muddling through the darkness of motherhood. Show me when I'm skating along the surface of life, ignoring pain's lessons. Teach me the importance of the lament's fulcrum—prayer. Turn my lament to praise, Lord, even today.

37

THE SEAGULLS
AND THE MAN

Clee

PERHAPS YOU'VE READ the book *The Old Man and the Sea.* Let me share with you a story I encountered today—something I'll call *The Seagulls and the Man.* Patrick and I took the children and our bikes to a nearby park that had a cement trail meandering around a man-made lake. Sophie, Aidan, and I circled the lake while Julia puttered along on her pink princess bike and Patrick circled her in his inline skates. Julia was quickly bored with the whole going-around-in-circles thing, and being a distracted child by nature, she felt compelled to stop and watch the ducks at the lake's shore.

Eventually, after our noses pinked and our ears screamed from the cold January day, we joined Patrick and Julia. January is a great time to watch birds in Texas because we see all kinds—honking Canada Geese, long-necked cranes, and brown nutty ducks all making circles in the water beneath the blue sky.

But what heartened me was seeing the seagulls. Sure, in my hometown of Seattle, they call the things "rats with wings," but seeing them quickened a brief nostalgia for home. Soon, a man came along with a brown bag. Instead of stopping on the lake's shore, he threw pieces of bread as he walked, so that the birds—

particularly the scrounging seagulls—followed him Pied Piper-like, croaking "Mine! Mine! Mine!"

He walked. They followed. And then, as it is with all things, his bread tossing came to an end and the birds dissipated to all corners of the world. Only a few trusty mallards strayed behind.

I turned to Patrick. "Isn't that a lot like Christians?" I asked.

"What do you mean?"

"Well, we're like those seagulls, aren't we? We chase after God as long as he gives us what we want. The moment he stops throwing bread, we leave him. Turns out, we were never really interested in knowing him, just his gifts."

Sophie was listening to our conversation. She seemed to understand what I was getting at. But she took it deeper. "Yeah," she said. "And then the seagulls find another person who has food."

I pray I am not a fickle seagull. I hope I don't run to other things when God's hand of blessing withdraws. I'm afraid, though, that I do. As quickly as a seagull spreads its utilitarian wings and lifts on the wind, I am eager to abandon God for other gods. The other gods don't have pagan names; they have names like success, popularity, materialism, and perfectionism. I set my heart on having an ideal Christian family. So often I run after things I think will fill me up, only to be wanting afterward.

I chase success and popularity, but when they come, I see higher rungs to climb.

I chase material things, but when I taste of them, my eyes look still farther ahead, wanting to put more things in my shopping cart.

I chase perfectionism until I realize I'm running along like a crazy hamster on a wheel, getting nowhere, exhausting myself.

I chase after the ideal Christian family, only to find out it doesn't exist and my striving for it is more about my pride than my spiritual maturity.

All these gods I chase after. All of them wear me out. None of them gives me grace. Like the fickle seagull, I have given much of my life in pursuit of things that will eventually run out. I have forsaken my relationship with God for things that never satisfy.

May it be that I flock to the One who gives me strength, instead of flying to those things that never fill me up.

Lord, show me where I have forsaken you for other gods. Show me where I've tried to be satisfied in other pursuits. I want to be one who flocks to you—purely for the sake of being with you and not merely for the bread that falls from your hand. Fill me today with your strength, Lord, and forgive me for turning away.

38

COVERED IN
HIS DUST

AY YOU BE COVERED in the dust of your rabbi!
This is a prayer by a sage in the *Mishna*—the entire body of Jewish religious law that was passed down orally and then transcribed. Rabbis in biblical times had followers or disciples. Being chosen by a rabbi was a special privilege. Students chosen to study under a particular rabbi spent every waking hour in the rabbi's presence. The followers formed small communities that followed the rabbi everywhere. The prayer comes from this idea: the rabbi's disciples followed so closely they were covered from the dust kicked up from his sandals.

Fast-forward a few thousand years. Today, the only dust we see is what collects on our end tables and television screens. Seldom are *we* dusty. But as mothers, we need to be. We've been granted the amazing privilege of being chosen by Jesus to be his followers. Jesus, the Rabbi of all rabbis, beckons us to follow him wherever he leads. As disciples, we are to hang on his every word, imitate his mannerisms, and spend our lives as he did. If we follow closely, we'll be covered in the dust of his sandals. What does his dust look like today? If he literally trod the paved streets of our neighborhoods and mounted the stairs to our homes, what would he do?

He would love the less fortunate. Many read the Sermon on the Mount and heartily agree with its upside-down kingdom metaphors—the poor are rich, the weak are strong, the hungry are filled, the persecuted are rewarded—but few of us engage the poor, weak, hungry, or persecuted. Insulated in our homes, the only time we see poverty or persecution is on late-night pleas for starving children. Jesus visited, touched, and redeemed the marginalized of society. If we are to be covered in his twenty-first century dust, we ought to pray he would send us to the hurting. The beautiful thing about that is not only does Jesus care for those less fortunate, but he *is* those less fortunate. He said, "I tell you the truth, whatever you did for one of the least of these brothers of mine, you did for me" (Matthew 25:40). When we serve others, we are serving him.

He would share the good news of salvation with whoever would listen. Often in the gospels, Jesus shares good news. He offends those who seem pious. He messes with a religious leader's supposed righteousness. He stoops low to the ground to scribble a message before telling an adulterous woman to sin no more. His message resonated redemption. As mothers, our words must sing with redemption—whether we're buying groceries, chatting with other mothers at the park, or volunteering in a classroom. To be covered in the dust of Jesus is to take on the mantle of sharing the good news with others.

He would let nothing get in the way of his worship of the Father. Jesus often pulled away to worship the Father and pray for wisdom and strength. He rebuked the Pharisees by saying, "I am telling you what I have seen in the Father's presence" (John 8:38). The words he spoke, the actions he performed, the tenderness he felt—all were a result of his time with the Father. As mothers, we live in a crazy-busy world where nanoseconds of time are efficiently used. Amid the blaring noise and rush, Jesus calls us to himself, just as the Father called Jesus to himself. We can only tell our children what we've seen in God's presence if we spend time there. Jesus said to worship God and love others. We cannot be covered in his dust if we fail to worship, if we fail to exalt him above every triviality of life. To be covered in his dust is to worship moment by moment.

Are you covered in his dust? Do you love the unlovely? Share the gospel? Worship the Creator? If you're anything like me, you walk life's path dustless. The truth is we can't walk near the dust of Jesus' sandals in our own paltry strength. We need his power within us to do these supernatural acts. And as we follow Jesus, we will serve as rabbis to our children—teaching them to love the unfortunate, share the good news, and praise God. As we follow Jesus, our children follow us. May they be covered in the dust that covers you.

Jesus, I want to be covered in the dust of your sandals, but I am weak. I need your strength. Show me the marginalized, Lord. I don't want to be insulated from others' needs even though I feel so busy. Help me to be brave and share the good news with others. I love you, Jesus, and I want to pull away to worship you passionately. As I do that, Lord, may my children be covered in your dust too.

39

Naked Barbie
Spirituality

GOD OFTEN GIVES ME METAPHORS through mother-hood, but I never expected that naked Barbies would make me think of him in a new light.

Today I was drying my hair when I noticed them—two blonde Barbies in their birthday suits, arms lifted to the heavens (or the bathroom ceiling). Seeing them like that, arms outstretched like my daughter Julia when she sings praises, made me rethink my day.

What struck me first was the Barbies' posture of praise. In the doldrums of life, unlike Barbie, I forget to lift my hands. When dishes beckon, floors stick to my shoes, and children's needs seem endless, I resign myself to tasks. But I don't do them willingly or happily.

I wish I could be like Brother Lawrence, who found the voice and delight of God in the mundane. Doing dishes was the Lord's work, and Brother Lawrence found a certain hand-raising delight in performing tasks with Jesus:

> We should offer our work to him before we begin, and
> thank him afterwards for the privilege of having done
> them for his sake. This continuous conversation would

also include praising and loving God incessantly for his infinite goodness and perfection.[17]

Brother Lawrence reminds me of the oft-quoted Scripture "Be joyful always; pray continually; give thanks in all circumstances, for this is God's will for you in Christ Jesus" (1 Thessalonians 5:16-18).

It is not always easy to be joyful when the laundry monster threatens to devour my home. It is not always easy to pray when the only time we have to think is the first three seconds in the bathroom (and even there, knocks and pleas break the silence). It's not easy to thank God when a toddler scribbles all over her naked body with Sharpie pens. But according to 1 Thessalonians, these practices are God's will.

I want to be like the Barbies—arms uplifted despite circumstance.

Aside from realizing I should lift my hands more, the naked Barbie metaphor prompted me to think of the Barbies' other state: nudity.

How often do I hide under clothing, makeup, or sunglasses? How often do I hide who I really am from the people I love most—my family? Oh, to be like pre-Fall Adam and Eve, living in that naked and unashamed state. I am a mother of shame, pelted by advertisements, books, and voices, screaming I am not enough. No wonder I cover myself. I need to protect my heart.

Fearful of being trampled, I am afraid to bear my heart to others. Sometimes I even fear laying bare my soul before God in unashamed abandon. If I did, I'd experience healing. I once heard a story about a pastor overloaded with counseling appointments. When counselees came in to see him, he told them to go to the sanctuary and pray for an hour. If they still needed his help, he'd be there to listen. Almost everyone left after a prayer-filled hour with God. I neglect to lay my heart naked before the Lord to my own detriment. I need to remember that the Wonderful Counselor waits for me, listens to my pleas, and heals my needy heart.

To be wholehearted followers of Jesus, we need to be naked before him. When we pour out our insecurities, sin, and inadequacies at his feet, he lifts our heads and hearts and places his robe of forgiveness gently around our shoulders. He, Love personified, died on the cross as a naked Man. Without clothing, without covering, in utter shame, he suffered for us. He understands a naked heart. And he loves to cover it with his grace, forgiveness, and strength.

Still, we groan for more, don't we? Many of us lament our groaning when we should welcome it. Our groaning is a sign that we are the Lord's and that someday, we'll be fully clothed and our nakedness will be covered for eternity.

"Meanwhile, we groan, longing to be clothed with our heavenly dwelling, because when we are clothed, we will not be found naked. For while we are in the tent, we groan and are burdened, because we do not wish to be unclothed but to be clothed with our heavenly dwelling so that what is mortal may be swallowed up by life" (2 Corinthians 5:2-4).

want to be a naked Barbie for you, Lord. I choose today to lift my hands to you, even amid the mundane tasks of motherhood. I give you my nakedness, my utter neediness for you. Help me to realize that someday the nakedness I feel in this life will be clothed with a robe of righteousness in heaven. Help me to do every task today in light of eternity.

40

TIME TO DO
THE DISHES

OE TO YOU, teachers of the law and Pharisees, you hypocrites! You clean the outside of the cup and dish, but inside they are full of greed and self-indulgence. Blind Pharisee! First clean the inside of the cup and dish, and then the outside will also be clean" (Matthew 23:25-26).

I read this verse sitting in my bed, anxious to hear the voice of Jesus. But something perplexed me. I could picture someone dusting the outside of a cup, or even using window cleaner and a diaper to polish its outside. But, I didn't understand how if I cleaned the inside the outside would appear clean too. Was the cup transparent? How could a shining inside be reflected on the outside?

Then I remembered my favorite task: doing the dishes. Truth be told, I'd rather pull my hair out strand by painful strand than wash dishes. It harkens me back to childhood where I, as an only child, stood on a stool and washed each greasy dish, rinsed every fork, and stacked them haphazardly in the dish drainer to the right of the sink. As I write this, my own children are whining downstairs. "Why do we *have* to do dishes?" asks one. "I'm not very good at dishes," adds another. "I don't have to do *every-thing*," one whines.

If I consider the dreaded chore of dishwashing, I realize that if I have a dirty cup—filthy on the inside and out—it becomes entirely clean when it is *immersed* in the sudsy water. That's what Jesus wants from me—to be immersed in his healing and cleansing waters. Only then will I be fully clean. Only then will others benefit from my cleanliness.

Jeremiah 2:13 reveals our propensity to run from his cleansing, refreshing water: "My people have committed two sins: They have forsaken me, the spring of living water, and have dug their own cisterns, broken cisterns that cannot hold water." Perhaps this is what the Pharisees did when they tried to beautify their outsides: They dug their own inefficient cisterns.

Unfortunately, I have a syndrome when I hear about Pharisees. I think, *Well, yeah, those awful Pharisees were hypocrites. Jesus reserved his worst criticism for those self-righteous folks. Of course they cleaned just the outside of their lives. Of course they dug leaky cisterns. They are so bad.* I forget that my heart looks an awful lot like a Pharisee's. I forget that too often I am digging wells in my own strength—living life my own way for my own glory—only to find the wells wanting. Instead of turning to his well, where all motivations and ambitions can be washed, I turn away and continue to dig holes, hoping this next one will hold enough water to satisfy me.

His water is living. His water, if we are immersed in it, will clean our insides so well that our outsides will reflect him to our families and the dying world outside our front doors. In John 4:13, Jesus answered the woman at the well, "Everyone who drinks this water will be thirsty again, but whoever drinks the water I give him will never thirst. Indeed, the water I give him will become in him a spring of water welling up to eternal life."

When my cup is dirty—full of anger, resentment, mommy-fatigue, impatience, hatred, and futility—I only need to drink from the fount of Living Water, Jesus. In the Jeremiah passage, the prophet speaks of forsaking living waters. May it be while I (joyfully!) do the dishes today, I remember my tendency to run from his living water—to hew cisterns of my own making instead of jumping headlong into his cleansing presence. May it be that I take that leap into the suds of his cleansing, so that he can wash me, inside and out.

Lord, wash me inside and out. Help me to remember your cleansing today when I do dishes— that I need to be immersed in you if I want abundance. Only you satisfy. Lord, forgive me for living life in my own strength today—for digging cisterns that leak. Fill my cup with your cleansing water today, and spill over my cup's lip to the lives of my children.

41

PLAYING ROCK, PAPER, SCISSORS — ALONE

ODAY FIVE-YEAR-OLD JULIA decided to play rock, paper, scissors by herself, using both hands. If her left hand *happened* to be scissors and her right hand paper, she'd cut her right hand with her left-hand finger scissors. Although she seemed content, I knew that eventually she'd tire of playing her solitary game, just as my other daughter grows frustrated when she attempts cat's cradle by herself. Life is often more fun when you have a friend.

How many days do I tackle the chores of motherhood alone? How many times do I play rock, paper, scissors with myself, forsaking the company of other adults? Isolationism easily creeps into a stay-at-home mother's life. With daily tasks, children who need much of our attention, and houses that don't clean themselves, sometimes the only time we venture out is for rudimentary things like buying milk, getting the oil changed, or making deposits. Chatting with the bank teller, however, does not qualify as community.

We've bought into the lie that we can be perfectly balanced mothers outside of community, when in reality we cannot exist without the warm embrace of the body of Christ. We need to let other women sharpen us like iron sharpens iron. We need mentors who encourage us in our feeble attempts at motherhood, who come alongside and say, "I've been there. Hang in there. God will pull you through." We need other mothers who face our daily life, so we can encourage each other and pray transparent prayers like, "Lord, help me to lower my voice when I'm angry" or "Lord, give me wisdom when my emotional preteen confounds me."

Hebrews 10:25 says, "Let us not give up meeting together, as some are in the habit of doing, but let us encourage one another—and all the more as you see the Day approaching." As mothers, we constantly live under a cloud of guilt, especially when it comes to the words "quiet time." We berate ourselves for our own lack. Amid that self-pummeling, we forget that not only are we to fellowship deeply with the God of grace (who does not act as a policeman in the sky every time our Bible is closed), but that he gives us bits and pieces of himself, his wisdom, his peace, his joy, and his grace through other believers. We feel bad when we don't meet him in prayer or regularly read the Bible, but seldom do we understand how important it is for our spiritual lives to be in community with other believers.

Christianity, and motherhood, too, should not be lived in isolation. Both are meant to be a communal experience. We encounter more of the God of the universe through others than if we putter through life alone.

As an only child, I had that unique longing for brothers and sisters, a longing only fulfilled when I came to Christ and realized he had populated the most surprising places with brothers and sisters. Somehow, though, when my children were in the throes of babyhood and toddlerhood, I forgot to meet with others as much. So wrapped up was I in the life of my children that I forgot how refreshing other Christians could be. When left to myself, I became sullen, exhausted, and graceless toward myself. At times, I resented my children.

Only within the context of community was I able to understand that I was not alone in my feelings as a mother. Within a small group of women, I was able to let out my pain and be prayed for. Slowly, the isolation faded, replaced by community.

Next time you see your children play rock, paper, scissors, remember. It's more fun to play with others. Mothers need the body of Christ—Jesus with skin on.

Lord, forgive me for living in isolation and not pressing into other relationships. Sharpen me through others today. Remind me to call a friend when I am worn out. Help me to offer grace to a graceless mom. Help me to know more of you through the people you've created so I can be a joyful mom.

42

POTEMKIN VILLAGE

I GET A VOCABULARY WORD OF THE DAY sent to me via email. It's been fun learning unfamiliar obscure words: rumbustious, lability, pinnate, trunnel, orotund, tsuris, kvell, parlous, swivet, and alienist.

One day the vocabulary mavens sent "Potemkin village," an impressive showy façade designed to mask undesirable facts. Herein lies the story behind the phrase.

Once upon a time, when the United States was an infant nation, a Russian army officer named Prince Grigori Aleksandrovich Potemkin (1739–1791) fell in love with a great lady, namely, Catherine the Great. In addition to being an officer and a lover—think Officer and a Gentleman eating borscht—Potemkin was a statesman.

Legend has it that when Catherine the Great planned a visit to the Ukraine and the Crimea in 1778, the prince decided the area needed a little sprucing up. So he created temporary villages to line the paths of her trip. He erected elaborate cardboard houses that appeared to be full of opulence and splendor. With deftness of a Hollywood set designer, he created prosperity where there was none.

Just like a Hollywood set whose street fronts don backless stores, ale-less saloons, and horseless livery stables, Potemkin's elaborate show was an illusion. Unlike Hollywood sets, however, his pretend villages covered up more than empty streets; the villages masked each community's abject poverty and filth. Behind cardboard homes of beauty, the real people who populated the towns Catherine supposedly waved to were living in squalor.

I, for one, do not want to be a Potemkin village. I want others to see me as I am—with faults, problems, joys, wrinkles, and pain just like the rest of the world's citizens. If the Catherine the Greats of the world want to parade on by, well, let them see me as I am—no whitewash, no showy façades, no elaborate sets.

Like David, I cry out, "Surely you desire truth in the inner parts; you teach me wisdom in the inmost place" (Psalm 51:6). I want my outside to match my inside, living a life free of hypocrisy.

Unfortunately, our homes are daily bombarded by the ultimate Potemkin village: TV. The television projects large doses of unreality, hiding the truth. If we were to believe TV to be a purveyor of truth, we'd have to conclude that nearly everyone was happily single or unhappily married or a hen-pecked, dimwitted parent. We'd have to believe the myth that beauty equals glory, that money equals worth, that youth equals respect, and happy rebellion equals good self-esteem.

TV is the penultimate Potemkin village—showing life as it is not, but as if it were. It tells us our problems must be solved or laughed away in 30-minute increments. It tells us happiness lies solely within ourselves, reducing kindness and selflessness to sappy greeting card commercials. It preaches crudeness over restraint, airbrushed superficial beauty over ageless inner beauty, and selfish ambition over considering others more important than oneself.

Thankfully, we have the option of turning off the switch—not only to television, but movies, radio, and the Internet. We can shut our eyes to the crazy Potemkin villages around us, meditating on Scriptures such as "I will sing of your love and justice; to you, O LORD, I will sing praise. I will be careful to lead a blameless life—when will you come to me? I will walk in my house with blameless heart. I will set before my eyes no vile thing. The deeds of faithless men I hate; they will not cling to me" (Psalm 101:1-3).

If we want a dose of reality, all we need to do is take a long look at our families—the one place Potemkin's touch should not reach. There, hopefully, lies a place where folks love us for who we really are, where they cheer even when we fail, where our foibles don't offend. In the crucible of family, we can dare to rip down the showy façades and revel in reality.

Besides, we'll never understand the deeper dimensions of love if we never allow a single soul to know who we really are, if we've perfected life behind a Potemkin village of our own construction. The village becomes an impenetrable wall to the people in our lives. True love is felt most keenly when we are at our worst—walls crumbled—and a loved one embraces us despite the rubble.

ear Jesus, tear down my Potemkin village. I want to be real. I want to understand the depth of your love for me, and I want to experience the reality of others' love for me. Help me to regulate the Potemkin village called TV that poisons my mind to your truth.

43

ONE GIRL,
THREE BROKEN ARMS

ULIA, OUR INTREPID FIVE-YEAR-OLD, broke her left arm today.

It's her third time.

She started breaking her arms when she was two, starting with her left arm, then her right, and now her left again.

We were sitting around our dining table eating dinner the first time she broke her left arm. That night I had boiled some corn on the cob. Julia loves corn on the cob—so much that she gripped the cob (once it was cooled) in her left hand. I think she harbored some sort of fear that if she didn't vise-grip the corn, some malevolent force would snatch it clear away, leaving her cornless.

She's never been one to sit straight in her chair. Being a silly-heart by nature, she flits this way and that, trading corners of her chair while chattering. Corn on the cob night was no different, except this time she lost her balance. Instead of letting go of the cob, she fell directly onto her left elbow, corn still gripped between her fingers.

I can still see her clutching the very thing that brought demise to her arm. How many of the cobs of corn that I grip bring me spiritual demise? I cling to anger and I reap a bitter heart. I grab onto jealousy and I inherit a thankless demeanor. I hold a grudge and gain a life of little hatreds. Remembering Julia, I need to ask the Lord, *What am I clinging to other than you? What do I hold that is poisoning my heart?*

In Julia's fourth year, one of Sophie's friends was helping her hold onto a pulley line and was pushing her very slowly from one end to the other. Problem was, the girl holding Julia was gripping her legs and when Julia lost her balance, her torso's momentum made her fall out of the girl's grasp.

As she fell, I realized the person holding her was not equipped to understand momentum or the fickle grip of little girls. Ultimately, I should have been holding Julia. As her parent, I understand her, and I am strong enough to keep her from falling. I learned I needed to let go of certain things when Julia broke her first arm. From this second fracture, I learned how important it is for us to cling first to our heavenly Father. He knows how to hold us. He understands the fickleness of his children.

Today, Julia stumbled down the latter half of our stairs, making the kind of noise that makes parents cringe. Tumble. Thud. Thud. Scream. This time, her left hand was hanging limply from her wrist, and we knew that once again we'd be heading to the hospital.

"Will I get a shot?"

"I don't think so," I told her.

Her tears calmed a bit while she bravely slipped on her shoes and went with Daddy to the ER. They x-rayed her birdlike left arm, found a buckle fracture above her wrist, and sent her home with a splint and an ace bandage, halting her kindergarten handwriting career for a few weeks.

When I saw Julia with her splinted arm, I hugged her and held her. I asked if she was brave.

"Yes, I was brave," she said.

"You really need to stop breaking your arms, Julia," I said.

"Yeah," she smiled. "I need to break my leg next!"

It's amazing to me she would say that—a pint-sized glutton for punishment, she is! But that is so much like us. We cling to things we shouldn't and let go of the Lord. Our sin creates havoc in our lives and still its lure is strong. We dare to walk down reckless paths. I am thankful that even in the midst of my waywardness, in my longing to "break my leg next," God still holds my hand (and Julia's!). "Though he stumble, he will not fall, for the LORD upholds him with his hand" (Psalm 37:24).

Lord, show me the things I cling to that damage my soul. Reveal when I have let go of your hand. Help me to stop running down reckless paths. Thank you that you hold my hand in this life. I can't live without you. I don't want to.

44

BROKENNESS

I FIRST HEARD ABOUT BROKENNESS from George Verwer, then head of Operation Mobilization—a young adult outreach and mercy mission's agency. He spoke at an Urbana conference where 18,000 missionary-wannabes hung on his every word. After hearing so many amazing stories about God's power in the world, Verwer surprised us by detailing his failures. He told us he was a hothead and that he yelled at people on occasion. He said that he had to learn the secret of confessing his sins and asking for forgiveness. He told us he learned that lesson in the school of brokenness.

Something in his words drew me. Brokenness. I've spent years since then trying to understand and embrace that word in my life, right down to my motherhood. There is a quote from the book *Calvary Road* by Roy Hession that illuminates my heart's propensity for pride and disdain for brokenness. As I read his words, I realize how far I am from true brokenness, even as I attempt to mother my children.

> As we look honestly at our Christian lives, we can see how much of this self there is in each of us. It is so often self who tries the Christian life (the mere fact that we

use the word "try" indicates that it is self who has the responsibility). It is self, too, who is often doing Christian work. It is always self who gets irritable and envious and resentful and critical and worried. It is self who is hard and unyielding in its attitudes to others. It is self who is shy and self-conscious and reserved. No wonder we need breaking. As long as self is in control, God can do little with us.[18]

How much of my parenthood is hard and unyielding? How often am I critical of my children or resentful toward my husband or envious of my friend? If I were to be honest, I'd have to say many of those words characterize me—particularly worry. I am so worried that I don't appear normal and together that I control my life. I control the façade others see. Yet none of that control is about humility or brokenness. It's about pride, about appearing to be perfect while my heart is full of hatred and pettiness.

I want to be more like George Verwer. I want to declare my shortcomings to my family, not in self-deprecating false humility, but in truth and candor.

"I was wrong when I raised my voice, Aidan. Can you forgive me?"

"I'm sorry, honey. This week I've lived life for myself and neglected you."

"Please forgive me, Sophie. You were right. I was wrong."

"Julia, I shouldn't have said those words. Can we start over?"

Jesus said if we fall on him, the Rock, we would be broken. "Everyone who falls on that stone will be broken to pieces, but he on whom it falls will be crushed" (Luke 20:18). Sometimes the only way our hardened hearts can be renewed is if Jesus breaks them open, laying them bare before his holy eyes. He promises not to crush our hearts to dust.

In that state where we are broken, seemingly beyond repair, Jesus does miracles. When we apologize to those we've wronged, he softens their hearts toward us. When we confess our sins before him, he cleanses us. He promises to be near to us. "The LORD is close to the brokenhearted and saves those who are crushed in spirit" (Psalm 34:18). But to the proud, the stiff-necked, the self-centered, he stays aloof. "Though the LORD is on high, he looks upon the lowly, but the proud he knows from afar" (Psalm 138:6).

Sometimes the world breaks me. Sometimes others' words rend my heart. Sometimes my penchant for sin makes me despair. The Broken One who bore every sin—whether committed against us or by us—waits with healing hands. He delights in humility because when we are in that state of desperation, we long for him more. May it be that we choose to let our hearts be broken so that they can be enlarged to hold more of him. May it be that desperation over our sin drives us to Jesus. May it be that our confessions before our families bring God his due honor.

Lord, I want to be broken before you and before my family. I don't want to live life only for me, only for my desires. Break me, Lord. Teach me to confess my failures. Pick up the broken pieces of my heart and make something beautiful of them.

45

WHEN YOU WRITE,
REMEMBER MIKE

MIKE SMITH SPENT HIS BIRTHDAY fixing our dryer. That's just the kind of guy he was. "I'd rather be helping you on my birthday than any other thing," he said with a wide smile, tools in hand.

I count it a supreme loss that I will never see that smile again on this earth.

One of the first times Patrick and I met Mike, he told us about a book he wrote, *The Secret*. It chronicled his harrowing story of nearly dying several years ago and his subsequent faith in God. Mike attended our Sunday school class, and although we were leaders of that group, we felt that Mike was teaching us more through his humble and cheerful heart than we could teach others in a lifetime.

He embodied the apostle Paul's words: "Do nothing out of selfish ambition or vain conceit, but in humility consider others better than yourselves" (Philippians 2:3). When our friend Keith was dying of brain cancer and his family needed yard work done, our Sunday school class pitched in. Mike came, even though by now he was suffering from complications of a failing liver and was very weak. Still, he dug small holes near the home's entrance and planted gladiola bulbs, bulbs that were blooming the day he died.

Before he went to speak at a church near his hometown, he suffered more complications, landing in the hospital again with internal bleeding. Instead of complaining, he said, "You know, I had been praying that God would keep my message about what I endured fresh. He answered my prayer by putting me in the hospital. The message is still fresh."

We prayed for him that day, and our group of folks cried—both for the suffering our friend was enduring and for the amazing ability he had to walk through trials cheerfully.

Mike emailed us the day of his liver transplant surgery. "Hi. It is just a little after 7:30 A.M. I just got the call and am about to head to Baylor for a [liver] transplant. The time has come to put my life in God's hand and let him do his will. Please pray for a speedy recovery and as few complications as possible. I love you all and wanted to tell you how important you are to me. God bless, Mike."

Our whole family visited Mike at the hospital. Our children laughed with him and listened to his stories as he awaited surgery. He was in good spirits, joking about how it took several hours for the nurses to get him a pillow. He said he was nervous and wanted us to pray for him. Our family encircled him, held hands, and prayed.

"Thank you," he said.

I wish I would have said, "No, Mike, thank *you* for showing me what love and compassion and grace and humility looked like. Thank *you* for your cheerfulness and patient endurance." Had I known it would be the last time I saw his dear face on this earth, I would have said so much more.

"I am in God's hands. If he wants to take me home, he will," Mike said before we left.

Twelve hours later, God took Mike home.

"I wake up every morning happy to be alive," he wrote in *The Secret*. "Life is indeed what we make it. We just have to trust in

God and believe there are things we will not know or understand. We should do the best we can to reach out to other people in need."[19]

After Mike's funeral, after my children wept and my eyes could leak no more, I sat absentminded at my computer. How I longed to honor Mike with my life. How I longed to mother in a way that exemplified his simple kindnesses, his humble love. How I longed to shine Jesus to a hurting world the way he shined it to me. As the curser blinked on and off, I heard the Lord say to me, "When you write, remember Mike."

I typed those words onto my screen and printed them off. They sit just above my monitor so I'll remember to honor Jesus with my writing. When I read them, I pray, *Lord, when I live and love and nurture, help me to remember Mike's gentle ways.*

In a world fraught with self-centered, me-seeking people, it's a rare thing to meet someone who defies explanation, who truly considers others more important. May it be that I become one of those people—in my home, in my neighborhood, in my extended family, in the world.

Lord, how I want to embody Philippians 2:3, but often I spend my days thinking only about myself. Turn my gaze heavenward. I want to love you and consider even my children as more important than myself. Send me examples, Lord, of people who live this way so I can see love tangibly demonstrated.

46

Jealous of
Unneeded Glasses

IN TENTH GRADE I ADMIRED a senior girl. She had every-thing: so many cute clothes I never saw her wear the same outfit twice, a trendy car, an equally trendy *and* sensitive boyfriend, a position on the cheerleading squad, and a kind disposition. She even had unneeded glasses.

When I saw her with them, I asked, "When did you find out you needed glasses?"

"I don't need them."

"What?"

"They're vanity lenses. I just think glasses are cool and wanted my own pink pair."

Suddenly, I pined for fake pink glasses. Other girls started showing up to school with unneeded glasses—all this in a farming community where kids aspired to work in the town's pickle factory, not exactly your bastion of cosmopolitan living. Economics prevented me from buying fake glasses.

When I tried on cheap reading glasses at the local drugstore, I realized there were two problems. One, I couldn't see with them. I couldn't afford real fake glasses, so if I tried a magnified alternative, I was subjugated to looking through a blurry world.

Two, the reading glasses looked like something Mrs. Claus would wear—not exactly the look I was after.

Fast-forward 20 years. I'm sitting in a church-planting seminar, unable to read the dry erase board. I justify it by thinking, *It's just the glare. Nothing more.* I nudged my husband. "Can you read that?"

"Sure," he said. Then he read the whole board, right down to the words he could read that had previously been erased. "Why?"

"Oh, I was just curious," I lied. Inwardly, of course, I thought I had a brain tumor. I'm one who thinks cancer is behind every spot, pain, and abnormality. *Well,* I reasoned, *I have had a good life. Here I come, Jesus.*

On my thirty-seventh birthday, I had my first-ever eye exam. The clinician prescribed driving glasses and gave me a clean bill of health otherwise. No cancer, thank God.

I've thought a lot about the curious juxtaposition of my desire to have fake pink glasses as a sophomore and my reluctance to wear needed corrective lenses as an adult. I've come to the conclusion that God doesn't give us what we think we want.

The spiritual principle is this: God doesn't always answer our prayers or give us our surface desires because we have limited perspective *and* he would rather fill our hearts with himself. Our desires are too weak. As C.S. Lewis said in *The Weight of Glory:*

> If we consider…the staggering nature of the rewards promised in the gospels, it would seem that our Lord finds our desires not too strong, but too weak. We are half-hearted creatures, fooling about with drink and sex and ambition when infinite joy is offered us, like an ignorant child who wants to go on making mud pies in a slum because he cannot imagine what is meant by the offer of a holiday at sea. We are far too easily pleased.[20]

What are the vanity glasses in your life? What is the one thing you must have to be happy today? Perfectly behaved children? A spotless house? An attentive husband? These desires are superficial at best. God wants to fill us with himself, with his presence amid bickering children, dirty toilets, and overworked husbands. Like Martha, we are distracted by wanting a well-run home. In the midst of that, we ignore Jesus. Mary, in her devotion, settled for the higher human need: intimacy with the Lord. According to Jesus, she chose the good part that wouldn't fade.

Now that I am wearing glasses, I laugh at my sophomore immaturity. I hear that voice in the back of my head that rails, "Be careful what you wish for—you just might get it." The glasses, though, are a good reminder.

To choose Jesus over superficiality.

To be careful for what I wish for.

To realize that I am getting older and not fight it.

With needed glasses, I see the beautiful world God created—in clear Technicolor. When I take them from the case, I am reminded that life is very short, I am getting older, and someday I'll see life as it really is. Someday, my weakened eyes will be perfect and I'll gaze at the face of Jesus unhindered. Oh, to live for that day. Oh, to embrace aging and choose the good part today.

Dear Jesus, help me to desire the deeper things of you. Help me to seek you before I seek to have my ambitions fulfilled. Help me to live for eternity. Give me clarity of vision to see what you would have me see in each pile of laundry, in each dirty dish.

47

TRUE JOY

Clee

OUR FAMILY LAUGHED and cried around a dining room table last week. The table held a pink cake with 46 candles. It took a heroic effort to light them all without matches burning flesh or candles waxing the cake. Still, wax dripped white and blue on pink frosting, but none of us seemed to mind. We were celebrating life.

The "we" was Patrick and me, our three children, and three friends—Denise, Katie, and David Willhite. They'd invited us over for dessert, for an evening of fellowship. We shared our presentation about going overseas to be church planters and answered questions about the upcoming move. We laughed. The kids played on David's new video game system. When we pulled away from the Willhite home, Julia said, "I want to go back there, Mommy. That was so much fun."

Before the pink cake was served, Denise said, "This is our first birthday without Keith. We wanted you to be a part of it."

The 46 candles represented the birthday Keith Willhite would have celebrated had he still been with us. However, his forty-sixth year is being spent in a place where time has little consequence and streets are paved with purest gold.

Brain cancer ebbed Keith's life last year, taking away an excruciatingly missed husband and father. Gathered around the blazing cake, we remembered Keith—his gentle ways, his heart for people, his great mind. David, his son, blew out the candles, and we ate cake—smiling as we remembered, but sad that we had to remember.

As pink frosting mustached Julia's lip, Denise said, "We have something for you. We decided to take the money we would have used to buy Keith a gift and give it to you—to go overseas. I know Keith would've wanted it that way." She slid an envelope over to Patrick. I caught Sophie's gaze, our tears welling simultaneously.

My mind flashed to a familiar story. Jesus watched as the crowd placed their offerings into the temple treasury. Rich folks threw in hefty amounts. Yet Jesus was drawn to a poor widow whose two tiny coins rattled in the offering—a pittance compared to the wealth given earlier. Jesus gathered his disciples and said, "I tell you the truth, this poor widow has put more into the treasury than all the others. They all gave out of their wealth; but she, out of her poverty, put in everything—all she had to live on" (Mark 12:43-44).

How often I forget that sacrifice means joy, that giving every ounce of myself to Jesus is what he requires. We often live life like hedonists—wanting absence of pain to be the prevalent drive in our lives—when Jesus praises the woman who risked deprivation for his sake. We think the "if onlys":

If only I had more money, then I would be happy.

If only my husband would praise me more, I would be thankful.

If only my children obeyed me the first time, I would smile.

If only I didn't have to sacrifice so much, I would be content.

True joy comes in surprising packages—in grief, in poverty, in suffering. It is primarily a hallmark of a soul bent on obeying Jesus no matter what the personal cost. The stories that move us are not "I made a million dollars. Look how great I am" but

"When he proclaimed his faith in Christ, his family disowned him."

As mothers, true joy peeks its head in while we do the mundane for the glory of God. We may not be offering a missionary our deceased husband's birthday money, but if we are giving everything we have to serve and follow Jesus, we are doing a similar act of worship. Mothers are often poured out for their children, and the reward seems small sometimes. We may labor in obscurity, without recognition, without fanfare. But if we serve Jesus wholeheartedly and seek to trust him, he will reward us— with joy, with the gift of his presence, with eternal treasures.

Moses experienced joy and God's presence as he looked forward to eternal treasures. "He [Moses] regarded disgrace for the sake of Christ as a greater value than the treasures of Egypt, because he was looking ahead to his reward" (Hebrews 11:26). We, too, must persevere, with hearts bent toward heaven, realizing our time on earth is short.

Keith Willhite is enjoying his reward as I write this. His wife and children are persevering through grief. They are storing up their own treasures as they treasure Jesus' presence. We, too, can do the same as we mother our children well, give Jesus everything we are, and endeavor to live selfless lives.

How selfish I am, Jesus. How often I think that getting more stuff or eliminating pain from my life is the means to happiness. I want to follow you. I want to give everything I am to you, particularly as I languish in motherhood. I need your holy perspective, Lord. Teach me to live for eternity.

48

ETERNAL PERSPECTIVE

I'VE BEEN THINKING ABOUT HEAVEN. A nurse at my doctor's office called saying my first-ever mammogram was abnormal and that I needed to have an ultrasound. Besides worrying about how we would pay for that, I fretted about the "C" word. I let my mind wander so far I could picture myself on my deathbed, touching my husband's face and telling him I wasn't ready to leave him. I saw myself giving my children last-minute motherly advice before I expired—all this from a faulty mammogram.

Since the age of ten, when I learned my father died, I have been afraid of death. Something about having a parent leave so suddenly made me spend nights staring at the ceiling, pondering the unknown void of death. I didn't know Jesus then. My mother's explanation later was that we live and die—when we die, that's it. Extinguished. No more you.

It wasn't until I met Jesus Christ at 15 that a tendril of hope wrapped itself around my fragile heart. I still feared death, but a peace settled into me that I couldn't explain. For years, though, I didn't think much about heaven. I longed for earth and what it afforded. I'd pray things like, "Oh please, Jesus, let me fall in love before you take me home" or "Just let me get married, Jesus, and then you can take me" or "I'd like to have a few children, Lord, before you call me heavenward" or "Would it be possible to have a book published before rigor mortis sets in?"

Like Abraham in Genesis 18, who pled with God about Sodom and Gomorrah, I pled with God about the span of my life, asking incrementally. Basically I was saying, "Please God, I want to really live life before I die. Please prolong it." I didn't understand what real life was all about. I didn't understand how amazing heaven would be. In my ignorance I believed this earthly life was all there is in terms of deep fulfillment.

Until I read Randy Alcorn's novel entitled *Deadline,* I had an ethereal view of heaven. I thought we'd float around in some sort of misty nirvana, not recognizing each other's forms and singing with angels all day long. It seemed to smack of all things tedious. Sing forever? Float forever in disconnectedness? Not exactly my idea of an interesting eternity.

After learning that heaven was a real place with real folks who were really whole, I got excited. There are times in musical worship that I get a tiny glimpse of how enraptured I'll be with Jesus in heaven. During intimate prayer times, his presence produces a guttural longing in me to be finally with him. When life just plain stinks, I have finally been able to say, "Okay, Lord, I'm ready."

But this week, with a bad mammogram haunting my thoughts, I haven't been able to say that. Perhaps God throws medical trials in our lives to reveal our hearts. I know in my case he did. My heart was pining for earth instead of longing for heaven. Yes, death is an enemy. Yes, we should fight it with all our vigor, but in the midst of that we must rest on God's incomprehensible sovereignty. He is God. He has numbered our days. He will be with us through trials—even health trials. I've considered Paul this past week. I have asked the Lord to help me utter Paul's words: "For to me, to live is Christ and to die is gain. If I am to go on living in the body, this will mean fruitful labor for me. Yet what shall I choose? I do not know! I am torn between the two: I desire to depart and be with Christ, which is better by far; but it is more necessary for you that I remain in the body. Convinced of this, I know that I will remain, and I will continue with all of you for your progress and joy in the faith" (Philippians 1:21-25).

This is a wonderful reminder to mothers. We can relax knowing that if we have to leave this earth, we will be much better off. If we have to stay in our hormonal bodies, God is good to provide fruitful labor for us. At this stage, as stay-at-home mothers, our labor takes on many forms—offering a cold cup of water in Jesus' name to a thirsty child, rearing our kids to become prayer mavens, investing in our children's hearts. No matter what our health situation, no matter how afraid we are of death, we can mother each day in light of eternity—doing things that matter both in this life and the life to come.

Dear Jesus, sometimes I fear death. I worry how my family would get along without me. Take away that fear, Lord, and replace it with a holy desire to make this day count for eternity. Elevate my thoughts about heaven so that my longing for it will color the way I love the people in my life today. When bad health news comes, help me to trust in you.

49

RUNNING WITH
SUN SHADOWS

*I*N THE MORNINGS before the kids leave for school, I go running. It's my time to be quiet and listen to God's voice. It's my time to have stillness. Sometimes it's my time to escape the hectic pace of our home.

This morning the sun seemed to follow me as I ran. It was early so the sun was low in the sky, its heat and light obscured by the tall houses lining the street. I shivered, trying to pick up my pace. Eventually I ran through an entrance to an alleyway where the sun found me, warming the side of my face. In that instant, it elongated my shadow making it reach from my side of the street to the opposite sidewalk. My shadow giant, I called it.

As I looked at my shadow giant, I realized something about our walk with the Lord. He is the sun. He makes our lives fuller, longer, more radiant. I'm just a little lump. He takes the light of his love and enlarges my lump into something magnificent. The lump is nothing—it's his light that makes it beautiful, significant. His light shines in our darkness, according to Paul. "For God, who said, 'Let light shine out of darkness,' made his light shine in our hearts to give us the light of the knowledge of the glory of God in the face of Christ" (2 Corinthians 4:6).

After his declaration of God's light, Paul likens us to a lump of clay that becomes a jar. He is quick to point out that the pot is nothing—it's what the pot contains that is important. "But we have this treasure in jars of clay to show that this all-surpassing power is from God and not from us" (verse 7). With the sun elongating my shadow, I realize the beauty and necessity for the sun. It is the reason for my shadow in the first place—therefore, it is preeminent. Just as an ordinary clay pot is nothing of import without its internal treasure, my life is dark without light. The treasure is Jesus. Without him, I have no treasure. Without light, I have no shadow.

Paul doesn't end his analogy there, though. Not only do we have the light of Christ, not only do we possess an amazing treasure in Jesus, but he gives us the ability to endure when life is hard. "We are hard pressed on every side, but not crushed; perplexed, but not in despair; persecuted, but not abandoned; struck down, but not destroyed" (verses 8-9). God gives us the ability to stand against the craziness of this world so that we are not crushed, despairing, abandoned, or destroyed. He elongates our hearts, stretching us with his power so we'll be able to persevere. Just as the sun followed me when I ran, the Son follows us as we run through life, helping us, keeping us company, giving us renewed vitality.

How much Jesus offers us! And yet, we forget the benefits of walking (or as in my case this morning, running) by his light. Why? Because we prefer shade to sun. We'd rather hide. "If we claim to have fellowship with him yet walk in darkness, we lie and do not live by the truth. But if we walk in the light, as he is in the light, we have fellowship with one another, and the blood of Jesus, his Son, purifies us from all sin" (1 John 1:6-7). If we fail to walk in his light, we have no elongated shadow and run cold and alone.

Next time you play hopscotch with your children and the sun angles your shadows across the pavement, tell them the story of Jesus. Tell them how he makes us so much more than we can imagine *if* we walk in his light. Tell them how his light is a treasure, that we're just pots holding his treasure. Share a story about how Jesus brought you through a trial. Share the benefits of "light walking" and caution them about a life without shadows.

And next time you're alone, walking to the rhythm of your own footfalls, welcome him. Let the Son shine upon you, elongating you, stretching your shadow to meet his light.

*M*ake sun shadows in my life today, Lord. *Elongate me. You are my treasure. You are my strength when trials knock on my door. I don't want to run in the shadows, Lord. Shine your white-hot light on my life right now so I can confess my dark sins to you.*

50

LESSONS FROM
A SNOWWOMAN

WHAT A WONDER SNOW IS!

We dreamed of a white Christmas this year—a dream yet to be fulfilled the six years we've lived in Texas. Instead, in a happy touch of irony, we celebrated a white Valentine's Day. You'd have thought it was the morning of the Jolly Old Elf. In that hazelike phase between deep sleep and morning sleep, I dreamt of voices. Dizzy-eyed, I puttered to the living room at 6:30 A.M. Three jumping children danced around.

"Snow!" said one.

"Look!" said another.

"Pretty!" said my youngest.

"It's six-thirty," I stated plainly. Without wonder—catching just a peek at the whitened earth—I turned and went back to my beckoning bed.

I regret doing that. Once again I was guilty of sleeping through wonder.

I redeemed the day when I rallied the children. "Time to make a snowman," I said.

My artsy sensibilities didn't like the fact that with only three inches of snow, grass poked out of every snowman ball. He was a hairy snowman—an odd thing since our children called her a snowwoman.

The hairy snowwoman donned metallic cheerleader pom-poms as ponytails. Julia, the owner of said pom-poms, protested at first. "I don't want the snowwoman to wear my pom-poms."

"But, Julia," Sophie encouraged, "won't she look pretty with pink ponytails? Like a princess?"

"If you put it that way, okay."

We used old CDs for eyes, giving our snowwoman that unforgettable Elton John look. For a nose, a carrot. For arms, two twiggy branches procured from a backyard tree in need of pruning. The snowwoman's mouth was a black plastic lei we secured with toothpicks. A crown and a sheer red scarf completed her eclectic ensemble.

This hairy snowwoman stood as a sentinel to our red-bricked home. When we drove through the neighborhood to critique the neighbor's snow creations, Hairy Snowwoman was our measuring stick. She stood taller than most—a point of pride for the DeMuth children.

We had to admit, though, that Perfect Man had us beat. We don't know Perfect Man's name. Every summer he has the most amazing lawn. Patrick and I both think he wakes up in the wee hours of the morning to hand clip each blade of grass. Perfect Man wins holiday lighting awards. I'm pretty sure if we had a snowman competition, his Perfect Snowman would have won—a cross between the Staypuff Marshmallow man of *Ghostbusters* fame, the Pillsbury Doughboy, and that legless Burl Ives snowman from *Rudolph the Red-Nosed Reindeer*.

No grass poked through his white façade. Instead of props, he was carved—even his hat and bulging eyes were carved. Like an ice carving from a Carnival Cruise, Perfect Snowman even dared to have an arm on his hip, daylight peeking clear through. He leaned on a cane. As we drove by, he seemed to wink at us.

When we drove home from church the next day, Perfect Snowman's fate reflected the others in the neighborhood.

Although most snow creations fell prostrate before the sun that melted them, Perfect Snowman still stood—but he leaned terribly.

"Let's drive by ours," Julia said.

Rounding the corner, we saw her—erect and smiling. Dirtied by grass, and missing one CD eye, she stood—not bending, not leaning, not bowing.

I smiled. We may not have a perfect lawn, but our homely snowwoman stood taller than the rest. Being a part of her creation with my snowball-throwing husband and my giggly children recaptured a bit of wonder for me. I realized there were spiritual truths attached to this snow adventure. We may not be perfect. We may have bits of dirt and grass protruding from our souls. We may be in need of cleaning, but his grace makes us stand. Maybe it's *because* we see our shabbiness that we see our need for Jesus to hold us up through life's trials. Maybe all the sticks and grass that pock our lives drive us to the feet of Christ. He is the only perfect Snowman. He's the only One who can remove the grass and dirt. And he's the only One who keeps us from falling headlong into the world's freshly fallen snow.

"To him who is able to keep you from falling and to present you before his glorious presence without fault and with great joy—to the only God our Savior be glory, majesty, power and authority through Jesus Christ our Lord, before all ages, now and forevermore! Amen" (Jude 1:24-25).

Lord, I'm afraid I'm not a pretty snowwoman. I've got character traits that look like sticks, rocks, and grass. Thank you for helping me stand even when I fail. Thank you for removing my sin as I approach you. More than anything, I want to stand for you.

51

THE IRRESISTIBLE FUTURE

I HAVE TROUBLE SLEEPING. One time, when Sophie was a toddler, I went three straight weeks without sleep. When I backed out of our driveway, I put the car in a ditch. Through my bleary days, I'd cry. Doing simple things like changing a diaper or making dinner seemed impossible. My hands disobeyed my head, fumbling and confused.

In the middle of the night, I would cry out to God. "Please, let me sleep. I'll do anything, Lord. Make my eyes shut. Make my mind turn off." That particular bout with insomnia was only broken by medication that made me feel like the bed was sucking me into it. In the morning, I had slept, but I had a hazy brain.

Because I struggle with falling asleep, when I do get a good night's slumber, I rejoice. Sleep is beautiful. Sleep is restorative. Sleep is a necessity. The Lord says that he gives to us while we sleep (Psalm 127:2 NASB). During insomnia phases, I looked up every verse about sleep and prayed through them, begging God for rest.

Then one day I cracked open *My Utmost for His Highest* by Oswald Chambers. Maybe I'd had a bleary-eyed night, maybe not, but his words struck a spiritual chord with me.

"Let the past sleep, but let it sleep on the bosom of Christ, and go out into the irresistible future with him."[21]

Let the past sleep. Sleep is characterized by unconscious activity. To let my past fall asleep is to let it slide into my unconsciousness. I have spiritual insomnia. I don't let my regrets, my failures, or my trials fall asleep. Instead, they are quite alive and alert, jumping on a trampoline in my mind as I rehash what I should have done. I berate myself for not loving my children enough or honoring my husband more. The past is awake. I can't seem to forget it.

But let it sleep on the bosom of Christ. Chambers offers a wonderful metaphor here. I can't seem to let my past sleep. An insomniac at heart, I can't (or maybe the better word is won't) let my failures rest. But there is something compelling about setting them upon the chest of my Savior—my Savior who took all my failures, sins, and weaknesses upon himself. I may not be able to let my past sleep just for the sake of sleep, but when I think about placing everything upon his chest, I think I might be able to do that. What I really want to do is place myself on his chest, to experience his restorative touch, to hear his whispers, to listen to the song he sings over me. Sheltered on his chest, I fall asleep to the rhythm of his heartbeat. Once asleep, once settled, I am able to finally let the past—even my motherly failures—rest. Jesus loves me. He shelters me. He holds me. He forgives me. On his great chest, I find rest.

And go out into the irresistible future with him. The only way to step out in faith is to let go of the past. Once I've let my past sleep on Jesus' chest, the future then seems irresistible because I face it alongside my Savior. With a freed heart—a heart no longer riddled with guilt—I am excited to see what happens next. I know I have failed as a mother. I have crushed my children's spirits. I have said angry words. I have spoken when I should have listened and listened when I should have spoken. Because I know I am forgiven, the voices telling me I'm a failed mother are silenced. I can view the future of my motherhood with joy, dancing on a clean slate, not being hindered by my past failures.

I'm reminded of Paul's words: "Forgetting what is behind and straining toward what is ahead, I press on" (Philippians 3:13-14). Motherhood is a journey. We stumble and fall. But God is there to take our guilt upon himself and enable us to walk forward with confidence.

Help me to place my past on your chest, Lord. I want to let it sleep there. Remove my guilt. Help me not to be held captive by my mothering failures. I want to walk with you, hand in hand, into the irresistible future.

52

PULL ONE WEED

Clee

WE START PLAYING the comparison game in preschool when someone has the disco Barbie we envy and move all the way through to adulthood when we pine for disco Barbie's impossible physique. My three-pregnancy body will never resemble airbrushed models—but I still compare. I also measure myself against holier women—women who resemble the perfect Christian woman. These perfect women have endless patience with their children and schedule "intimacy dates" with their husbands. They are room moms, carpool coordinators, menu planners, coupon clippers, and Bible study leaders. They seem to be able to do everything well.

I've come to understand, though, that the comparison game has no winners. Those women who appear to have everything lined up perfectly are just as harried and stressed out as I am. They fret about their lives just like I do. They struggle spiritually.

I used to think sanctification—that theological word that simply means becoming more and more like Jesus—was a linear process, progressing from initial faith to reading and memorizing the Bible to evangelizing every unsuspecting grocery clerk to finally ending in African missionary nirvana. But God's path for us, just like his creation, is diverse, organic.

One day God widened my linear view of sanctification. Jogging in my neighborhood I saw many yards—all different. Some had Yard of the Month signs. Others bred weeds. Others were manicured. The Lord spoke to me one morning as I jogged by two yards, one weedy, the other not. "Sanctification looks different for different people. Some people have more weeds to pull than others. Sometimes plucking one weed is enough."

Those women who appear to have manicured spiritual lives have different weeds to pull. Maybe their weeds are hidden behind a seven-foot fence. Maybe they've walked farther with Jesus than I have. Maybe they had upbringings that made it easier for them to trust God with the details of life. But, really, none of that matters. I am not their gardener, Jesus is. It's not up to me to weed someone else's yard. I am responsible (as I depend upon God) for my own.

The thought of picking my own unique weeds piggybacked on something a friend told me earlier that week. He said, "For a sexually abused child, now adult, just hugging her husband is sanctification." I resonated with that, especially since I compared myself to women who loved their husbands and children better than I seemed to be doing. As a sexual abuse survivor, I struggle to connect deeply and affectionately with my loved ones. Each hug I make is a step toward sanctification, even if a casual observer notes little change in my overall behavior. My yard may appear weedy to you. No matter. I just have one weed to pull at a time, and my weeds are different than yours.

If I play the comparison game, I shortchange God's unique sanctification plan for me. I may uproot weeds he intended to be thorns in my flesh. Sometimes God allows thorns to keep us wholly dependent on him; by trying to remove them, we remove his unique plan of discipline.

I may try to be a friendly neighbor and point out your weeds, placing myself firmly in the Gardener's place.

You may see my weeds and scoff.

Yet your weeds and my weeds are different because you and I are unique. We've walked different journeys. God is pruning the garden of our lives to bring him the most glory. Yours may be a neat French provincial garden. Mine may be a wildly overgrown English cottage garden, but both are worthy. Both are testimonies to the Gardener's skill. Both are in process. None are weedless.

The Message renders Galatians 5:26 this way: "That means we will not compare ourselves with each other as if one of us were better and another worse. We have far more interesting things to do with our lives. Each of us is an original."

Dear Jesus, help me to stop comparing my spiritual yard with someone else's. Enable me to be content with the gardening plan you have for my life. If thorns come to bring discipline, help me to bear them well. If there are tenacious weeds you want me to root out, give me the strength to pull. If my sister has a prettier yard than me, I pray that I would delight in it, attributing the amazing beauty to your dirt-stained hand.

53

BEWARE OF
PEDESTALISM

*"P*EDESTALISM" IS DEVASTATING to our relationships—with God and with other women. Its meaning, from the *D.U.D.*—the *DeMuth Unabridged Dictionary*, is to place ordinary women on pedestals, both for the sake of elevation and defamation. I've unfortunately been on both ends of the "pedestalism" phenomenon—a phenomenon that is fueled by the twin sins of jealousy and envy.

I've aggrandized mothers I've admired. This had two effects on me. First, I felt inferior because I fell short of my perceived notion of the unsuspecting woman. Second, I did the catty thing, catapulting myself back to those junior high days when girls knew just how to "love" the friends they were jealous of. I talked *about* her, maybe not to others, but enough to make my head a fertile breeding ground for mean, jealous thoughts. How easily I forget the slicing words of Proverbs: "Anger is cruel and fury overwhelming, but who can stand before jealousy?" (Proverbs 27:4)

So I elevated a mother for being successful and simultaneously defamed her for that same trait, neither of which made me feel any better. Aeschylus, the ancient Greek playwright, noted,

"How rare, men with the character to praise a friend's success without a trace of envy."[22] Perhaps the true mark of a friend is not whether she can weather the bad storms with you, but whether she can rejoice when you fabulously succeed. And telling her you're happy for her and then taking shots behind her back doesn't count.

Elevating anything or anyone above God is called idolatry. To the people of Israel, God said, "You shall not make for yourself an idol in the form of anything in heaven above or on earth beneath or in the waters below" (Exodus 20:4). Our jealousy may cause us to unhealthily elevate another woman, but in that we forget the jealousy of God. He will not allow other people to take his place. He continues, "You shall not bow down to them or worship them; for I, the Lord your God, am a jealous God" (Exodus 20:5).

In addition to "pedestalizing" other women, I've been on the receiving end of such envy as well. Once I received a letter from someone that detailed her struggle to love me because I had certain gifts and attributes that differed from hers. Although she wrote she loved me in the letter, I came away from the lengthy piece feeling misunderstood. Another woman pulled me aside once and confessed her jealousy of me. "I need to tell you I'm having a hard time liking you," she said. Another friend expected me to meet needs only the Lord could meet. She found out, much to her disappointment, that I made a lousy god.

"Pedestalism" hurts both parties. Although it's not wrong to admire godly women who have walked the path before you, it's important not to elevate them above Jesus in importance. Nor is it right to allow your heart to envy. Consider the convicting words of James: "If you harbor bitter envy and selfish ambition in your hearts, do not boast about it or deny the truth. Such 'wisdom' does not come down from heaven but is earthly, unspiritual, of the devil. For where you have envy and selfish ambition, there you find disorder and every evil practice" (James 3:14-16).

Jesus was delivered up to be crucified because of jealousy and envy. The Pharisees were envious of his abilities and their perceived "pedestalism" of him in the community. That is why Matthew said, "For he [Pilate] knew it was out of envy that they handed Jesus over to him" (Matthew 27:18).

The truth is, all mothers fail. We may look great on the outside. We may be admired or we may be jealous of other admirable women, but all of us fall short of Jesus' perfect love. We'd be better off placing Jesus on the pedestal—the throne where he belongs—and instead cheering and loving the women God places in our paths.

ord, forgive me for placing other women on a pedestal, for envying them, for gossiping about them to others or entertaining bad thoughts. Help me to place you on the throne. Keep my heart tender and receptive to your conviction. Enable me to cheer the women in my life who appear so perfect.

54

THE MYTH
OF PERFECTION

Clee

IN THE MIDST OF MY PURSUIT of God I've had several misconceptions, one of them being I thought the goal of sanctification was perfection—and I equated perfection with the Proverbs 31 woman, who woke up before a godly hour and knitted scarlet sweaters for everyone. In college I wanted to be like martyr Jim Elliot, so I memorized Scripture as I stood in line for lunch. Nothing wrong with that, of course, but it made me think Christianity was a checklist. Checking off "Memorizing Scripture like Jim Elliot" became yet another step in my journey toward being a Proverbs 31 woman.

I added more things to my checklist when I got married: prayer time together, consistent quiet time before I left for work, a spanking clean house. When I had birthed a few children, the list grew larger: prayer with children, squeeze in time with Jesus between diaper changes, save as much money as possible so I can be published in *Tightwad Gazette*. If I could just check these things off, I would become perfect. Maybe that's why the Proverbs 31 woman haunts me so much—because my list became unwieldy and unrealistic. Every time I fail, she is quick to whisper words like:

"Not going to her baseball game today will scar your child for life."

"So-and-so did a better job on that project than you did."

"You're becoming like _____!" (Place the name of a person you don't want to turn into here.)

"Look at your toilets! I would *never* allow such rims in my house."

"If you're not the room mom for every child, you are a failure as a mother."

Oswald Chambers in *My Utmost for His Highest* threw a wrench into my notions that the goal of sanctification is perfection.

"Christian perfection is not, and never can be, human perfection."[23] *Hmm, you mean I can't be perfect in my own human strength?*

"When you obey the call of Jesus Christ, the first thing that strikes you is the irrelevancy of the things you have to do, and the next thing that strikes you is the fact that other people seem to be living perfectly consistent lives."[24] *Oh, you mean like that pesky Proverbs 31 woman?*

"Such lives are apt to leave you with the idea that God is unnecessary, by human effort and devotion we can reach the standard God wants. In a fallen world this can never be done."[25] *It can't? But I've tried so hard.*

"I am called to live in perfect relation to God so that my life produces a longing after God in other lives, not admiration for myself…God is not after perfecting me to be a specimen in his showroom; he is getting me to the place where he can use me."[26] *Hmm, but I kind of liked being a pretty statue in your showroom, Jesus. You mean perfection has to do with my relationship with you, not my spiritual to-do list?*

The more I get away from spiritual to-do lists, the closer I get to marveling simply in his grace that covers all my sins and makes me perfect in his eyes. Thankfully, the closer I get to Jesus, I realize his voice is not that condemning voice I wrongly attributed to the

Proverbs 31 woman. He doesn't speak in condemning I-told-you-so tones. His is the voice of peace:

"Sure, you missed the game. Am I not big enough to fill your child's disappointment?"

"On that project? You did what I asked you to do. Well done."

"By the Holy Spirit's work in your life, you are becoming more like Jesus."

"Toilets, schmoilets. Playing Go Fish with your children is more important than white rims. Keep investing in your children!"

"Being a room mom doesn't necessarily bring you closer to me."

I've come to realize that sanctification is more about listening to his holy voice and heeding it than trying to do a bunch of things I think are holy. He is the One who sanctifies me. He will bring my wholeness and blamelessness about as I follow and trust him. "May God himself, the God of peace, sanctify you through and through. May your whole spirit, soul and body be kept blameless at the coming of our Lord Jesus Christ. The one who calls you is faithful, and he will do it" (1 Thessalonians 5:23-24).

Lord, I am tired of lists. Help me to run to you instead of lists. Help me to listen for your voice instead of the accusing voice. Instead of relying on my own faulty holiness, I choose today to run into your arms. You do the work, Lord. Teach me to rest in you.

55

GOD'S
TENDER VOICE

'VE LONGED TO HEAR the voice of God even as I sputtered my first prayer to him under an evergreen tree at 15. Somehow I knew, even then, that his voice was powerful. Consider what his voice can do: "The voice of the LORD is powerful; the voice of the LORD is majestic. The voice of the LORD breaks the cedars" (Psalm 29:4-5). Imagine someone's voice breaking a stout tree trunk as though it were a pencil. Powerful.

As I've walked closer with Jesus—through college, marriage, and motherhood—I've realized that this powerful voice is also tender, inviting. Like Elijah, I've listened for his thunder, only to be delighted by his soft wind:

> The LORD said, "Go out and stand on the mountain in the presence of the LORD, for the LORD is about to pass by." Then a great and powerful wind tore the mountains apart and shattered the rocks before the LORD, but the LORD was not in the wind. After the wind there was an earthquake, but the LORD was not in the earthquake. After the earthquake came a fire, but the LORD was not in the fire. And after the fire came a gentle whisper. When Elijah heard it, he pulled his cloak over his face

and went out and stood at the mouth of the cave. Then a voice said to him, "What are you doing here, Elijah?" (1 Kings 19:11-13).

Why can't we hear God's voice in the midst of our busy lives? Why can't we hear his whispers?

We are not quiet enough. If our days are spent amid the cacophony of children, the blare of music, the teaching of the radio, the flashing of the Internet, the whirring of TV, we will have to make a concerted effort to be quiet. Turn off the noise. Instigate an F.O.B. (Flat on Bunk) time with children so that the house is quiet at least one hour a day. Instead of filling the minivan with music, be content with the hum of the motor. At night when stars pock the sky, leave the cave as Elijah did, and feel the gentle breeze of God's wind.

We feel unworthy of hearing him. Because we are well acquainted with our sin, we feel ashamed to hear from God. Yet he promises that he is not an angry parent who scolds his children when they ask something of him. "If any of you lacks wisdom, he should ask God, who gives generously to all without finding fault, and it will be given to him" (James 1:5). God gives to us generously, and he loves to speak to us.

We have not taken the plunge. If we've contented ourselves with sloshing in mud puddles when the lake of his presence beckons us, we may have a hard time hearing his voice. We must freely dive into the things of God. Perhaps we are not hearing his voice because we have not fully given him everything—our future, our heart, our fears, or our children.

We don't fear God. God shares himself with those who fear him. We fear others. We fear the future. But we forget about fearing God. Just reading the 1 Kings passage about the raw power of God to create wind, earthquakes, and fires should cause our hearts to fear him in reverence.

Pride. Consider this verse: "Though the LORD is on high, he looks upon the lowly, but the proud he knows from afar" (Psalm

138:6). God is intimate with the humble but is distant from the proud. He does not speak to the proud-hearted. How can we as mothers get to that place where we dare to pull a cloak over our face, leave the cave, and hear God's voice in a gentle, life-recharging whisper?

Embrace humility. I appreciate how Jack Deere equates humility with hearing God's voice, "Humble people put their confidence in the Holy Spirit's ability to speak, not in their ability to hear, and in Christ's ability to lead, not in their ability to follow."[27]

Remember the tenor of God's voice. His voice is not the one that condemns, maligns, and ridicules. His always comes with truth and a huge dose of hope. Learn to discern which voice is speaking to you, taking "captive every thought to make it obedient to Christ" (2 Corinthians 10:5).

Be alert. The Lord may speak to you in odd moments—while examining a painting, watching a fire ant crawl across your toe, caring for a croupy child. Part of the key to hearing his gentle whisper is an expectant heart.

Lord, I want to hear your voice. I want to know you see me. I humble myself before you. Show me where I've given more credence to my ability to listen than your ability to speak. Help me to understand when you are speaking to me and help me to weed out the other voices, taking them captive. Give me an expectant, alert heart, Lord. I want to hear you.

56

THE PURPOSE
OF SUFFERING

Clee

I DON'T LIKE TO SUFFER. While my body was balled on the cold tile of a hospital ER waiting area, my children wondered if I were going to die. I thought I might. During five days of hospitalization, including an "inadvertent" overdose of Demerol by inattentive nursing staff, I passed two kidney stones. What could possibly come out of this horrific experience? Why do we have to suffer? What is its purpose?

Suffering makes us spiritually strong. "The God of all grace, who called you to his eternal glory in Christ, after you have suffered a little while, will himself restore you and make you strong, firm and steadfast" (1 Peter 5:10). During a difficult time in our marriage, I leaned on the Lord. He pulled me through that time because in my own strength I was desperately weak. I learned the paradox that "when I am weak, then I am strong" (2 Corinthians 12:10).

Suffering silences the devil. Even when no one is around to witness our suffering, our response to it is a holy declaration to the principalities that our allegiance is to God. Joni Eareckson Tada in *When God Weeps* said, "The life of the most insignificant man is a battlefield on which the mightiest forces of the universe converge in warfare."[28] Alone in an MRI tube—the ceiling one inch from my eyes—I silenced the enemy by thinking praise songs.

Suffering makes us like Jesus. "I want to know Christ and the power of his resurrection and the fellowship of sharing in his sufferings, becoming like him" (Philippians 3:10). Our friend Mike died last year. He suffered from incurable liver disease. During one relapse, he thanked God for the opportunity to suffer. Of all the people I've known the past several years, it wasn't the strong or capable who reflected Jesus—it was Mike and the inauspicious, humble manner he possessed as he endured suffering.

Suffering makes us long for heaven. Joni Eareckson Tada says, "Suffering keeps swelling our feet so that earth's shoes won't fit."[29] The more we live, the more we suffer. The more we suffer, the more we pine for heaven. The more we pine for heaven, the more we live in light of its reality.

Suffering enlarges our ministry toward others. "Praise be to the God and Father of our Lord Jesus Christ, the Father of compassion and the God of all comfort, who comforts us in all our troubles, so that we can comfort those in any trouble with the comfort we ourselves have received from God. For just as the sufferings of Christ flow over into our lives, so also through Christ our comfort overflows" (2 Corinthians 1:3-5). I love the juxtaposition of the words *all* and *any*. God comforts us in *all* our troubles. His comfort then qualifies us to minister to those in *any* trial. God's comfort in the midst of suffering is his baccalaureate program, readying us to minister to others.

Suffering keeps us thankful. Samuel Johnson said, "It is by affliction chiefly that the heart of man is purified, and that the thoughts are fixed on a better state. Prosperity, unalloyed and imperfect as it is, has power to intoxicate the imagination, to fix the mind on the present scene, to produce confidence and elation and to make him who enjoys affluence and honors forget the hand by which they were bestowed."[30] Affluence and prosperity make us forget our Creator. Suffering reminds us of our need and dependence for him.

Suffering is universal. It invades every aspect of our lives, including our homes. Yet, as protective mothers, we often try to shield our children from suffering. We'd rather they be insulated from the pain of this world. While protecting children is vitally important, it's equally important to allow for God's great school of suffering to refine our children. Suffering will drive them to their knees, especially if we have modeled that same response.

I homeschooled Sophie until second grade. In public school, she longed for a Christian friend. She was lonely and scared. She came home day after day, saddened that she couldn't find a friend. She prayed. I prayed. The family prayed. In a few weeks, she met Kate—a Christian girl who is still her best friend today. Had I rescued Sophie from school, she wouldn't have learned how to use her suffering as a springboard to trust Jesus.

I don't like to suffer, Lord, but I would like to suffer well. Show me the beauty of suffering, and help me to model suffering that glorifies you. I long to protect my children. Give me discernment to know when I am shielding them from the lessons you have for them.

57

THAT RESTLESS EVIL

*G*OSSIP. WE ALL DO IT. We all think it doesn't really matter. We don't equate it with murder or adultery, but it is as deadly. There was a time God asked me to consider my tongue, and he has not let me stop considering it. I remember first hearing about the tongue at a retreat. I was 20 years old. The speaker opened her Bible and flipped through it so we could see its marked pages.

"I mark my Bible in colors. Green is for anything relating to the tongue." While she fanned her Bible, green underlines were everywhere especially in the book of James. A section she read to us stood out to me: "But no man can tame the tongue. It is a restless evil, full of deadly poison. With the tongue we praise our Lord and Father, and with it we curse men, who have been made in God's likeness. Out of the same mouth come praise and cursing. My brothers, this should not be" (James 3:8-10).

I used to think my tongue was tamed, especially when I met someone whose tongue was not. For weeks I felt the Lord wanted me to confront this person. In the midst of that, the Lord kept reminding me of the log/splinter metaphor. How could I confront someone with a mouth sin if I practiced the very same thing? During that excruciating time, the Lord illuminated my own propensity to

- Talk negatively about people out of earshot.

- Slander public leaders even when I didn't know the true story.

- Tear down my brothers and sisters in Christ all the while making it sound as though I were merely "concerned" for them. How nice of me to work out their problems with other folks!

- Complain—about my hair, the weather, money, a sales clerk, a stomachache, my whining children, my husband's tardiness, the "stupid" driver in front of me.

- Judge other people's motives.

- Gossip about someone's misfortune.

- Hate those who were different from me. (I didn't call it "hate," of course, but by my actions and the way I looked at certain people, it was hate.)

- Tell a coarse joke.

- Extend forgiveness to some, but neglect to extend it to others.

- Get in the middle of someone else's business not intended for me.

- Express secrets, even though I knew they were probably meant to remain secrets.

- Share prayer requests for other people who probably didn't want their news advertised.

- Discuss difficulties in our marriage without first discussing them with my husband.

Amid this painful introspection, I realized how very dark my heart was and how I'd let slander and gossip take such a root in my heart that I barely recognized it as sin. As God illuminated my sin, I got to the point that I became so sensitive to anything smacking of gossip that I couldn't read the inside page of the Sunday paper's *Parade* magazine because it highlighted celebrity gossip.

I thank God that he enabled me to see the splinter in my friend's eye (mouth!) because had he not, I wouldn't have known my propensity to hurt others and pain God with my mouth. Gossip and slander are serious sins. Just because entire industries are based on celebrity gossip does not excuse us from taking this sin seriously. Little eyes are watching me. Little ears listen to me. How I speak of other people will be how my children speak of their friends and enemies.

We must follow the sage advice of Paul: "Do not let any unwholesome talk come out of your mouths, but only what is helpful for building others up according to their needs, that it may benefit those who listen. And do not grieve the Holy Spirit of God, with whom you were sealed for the day of redemption. Get rid of all bitterness, rage and anger, brawling and slander, along with every form of malice. Be kind and compassionate to one another, forgiving each other, just as in Christ God forgave you" (Ephesians 4:29-32).

Lord, illuminate my mouth. Show me where I gossip, slander, and humiliate others with my words. Help me to see how restlessly evil my tongue can be. Teach me to listen more, to hold my tongue, so that my children will have a good example to follow. Forgive me, Lord.

58

OUR PRIMARY
MINISTRY

Cee

*I*HAVE BEEN WRITING IN JOURNALS since sixth grade. Perhaps it was because I was an only child and I needed a place to vent my feelings, to be listened to. Sometimes, as a spiritual exercise, I revisit my journals to see how far the Lord has brought me or to discover those places I am still struggling through.

The January 2, 1998, entry caught my attention:

> Another thought came to me yesterday. What occupation is there that only I can do? I am uniquely qualified and gifted to be a mother to my children. Any other endeavor pales in importance. Perhaps someday I will go to seminary and be in ministry. As of now, my husband and children are my primary ministry. Oh Lord, give me true joy in that. Help me to do the work of an evangelist and fulfill my ministry. Give me stamina, cheer, and purpose in it, Lord.

As a stay-at-home mom, I struggle with significance. I can hear bits of that struggle in the journal entry. Loving my husband and parenting my children aren't the markers of a huge crusade ministry. As I clean the kitchen and make beds, I am reminded of the lessons of obscurity. As I help my daughter with her science homework, I am shaping a future leader. Holding a child as he vomits—as my own stomach churns at the sight and smell—is a blessed proving ground for ministry. Jesus, after all, said we must be servants if we want to be first. The greatest are the stooped. The humble are exalted.

The words in my journal ring true. My primary ministry is to my husband and children. They are my congregation, the ones God has entrusted me to minister to. If I fail to make them a priority, I will have failed on a fundamental level. I will have despised the days of humble beginnings. Jesus said when we pray or give, we should hide away, proving that much of spirituality is an unseen act. Motherhood is such an act. I am often unseen. I am not often applauded.

Consider Jesus. He poured his very life into 12 men. Those 12 men, through the power of the Holy Spirit, turned the world upside down. We have a similar task. I may not have 12 children, but I do have three. I can make it my ambition to love them well, to show them Jesus, to push them out of the nest when independence beckons, to teach them about life and conflict and joy. They, in turn, will leave my little "school of discipleship" and possibly change the world.

Even before the enormity of the motherhood task, I am called to devote myself to my husband. As high a priority as my children are, my husband is still my primary ministry. God has blessed me with a wonderful man, but sometimes in my quest to mother my children or pursue my own dreams, I neglect to build into Patrick. I forget to honor him with my words.

I love him selfishly—in the manner I like to be loved. He's a physical touch and words of affirmation guy (thanks, Dr. Smalley). I, on the other hand, adore little romantic, encouraging notes. I write them to Patrick, but for some strange reason, they don't minister to him as much as a passionate kiss or an "I'm proud of you."

I give all my energy to our children, or housework, or bills and have nothing left to give.

I complain about my life at home.

I let myself embody "frumpy housewife."

I nag.

Yet the Bible says, "A wife of noble character who can find? She is worth far more than rubies. Her husband has full confidence in her and lacks nothing of value. She brings him good, not harm, all the days of her life" (Proverbs 31:10-12). I hope I can be a wife of noble character who does good to my husband all the days of my life. In doing that, I honor Jesus who gave his life for me. In serving Patrick and my children, I am serving Jesus.

Lord, help me to not despise my primary ministry—my husband and my children. I want to revel in what you have to teach me while I stay at home. Help me to be faithful in the unseen things. Help me to disciple my children and love my husband well.

59

BREAD-MAKING

E TOLD THEM STILL ANOTHER parable: 'The kingdom of heaven is like yeast that a woman took and mixed into a large amount of flour until it worked all through the dough'" (Matthew 13:33). My husband jokes that my first loaf of bread could be used to build a brick fireplace, it was so hard. Still, he ate it—chewing and chewing until he dutifully swallowed the mealy lump. For years, bread-making was an elusive art, something mastered only by folks wearing tall white hats.

Me? Well, I made bricks.

It wasn't until Eva came into our lives that I understood what I was doing wrong. For the month after our second child was born, Eva cleaned, entertained my oldest, let me nap, and made amazing bread. She taught me that I needed to "proof" the yeast—let it sit in a warm, sweet liquid until it bubbled. She gently told me I was under-kneading. She showed me how to beat and push the dough into submission for 15 minutes.

"See here? It needs to feel like this." She gave the dough a good spank. "When it's done it should feel like a baby's bottom."

I smacked the dough. Sure enough, it did feel like an undiapered rump.

"You need to work the yeast and gluten all the way through the dough until it's no longer tough, but stretchy." She showed me how to do the windowpane test, stretching the dough so I could see through it. If it ripped before the windowpane appeared, it wasn't yet ready and I would have to punch and pound it more.

Thanks to Eva, I now make high-rising bread, and my husband no longer has to chew until his teeth hurt.

I realized my bread-making journey is a lot like spiritual growth.

We need tenacity. It took me four years to perfect my first loaf of bread. Following in the footsteps of Jesus requires a similar endurance. Upon failing, we need to go forward even if we're discouraged or disheartened. Paul encourages, "Let us not become weary in doing good, for at the proper time we will reap a harvest if we do not give up" (Galatians 6:9).

We need to knead longer. So much of life consists of convenience and instantaneous gratification. If we expect this in our spiritual life, the end result will be dry, hard spirituality. We need to allow the Bread of Life to knead his gluten and yeast into our hearts. His kneading hurts, but it yields high-rising spirituality and hearts that stretch. Peter describes our spiritual journey in terms of adding ingredients (qualities). Adding character traits takes discipline and time. "Make every effort to add to your faith goodness; and to goodness, knowledge; and to knowledge, self-control; and to self-control, perseverance; and to perseverance, godliness; and to godliness, brotherly kindness; and to brotherly kindness, love. For if you possess these qualities in increasing measure, they will keep you from being ineffective and unproductive in your knowledge of our Lord Jesus Christ" (2 Peter 1:5-8).

We need mentors. I didn't understand how well-kneaded dough was supposed to feel. I needed the expertise of someone who understood bread-making, and I needed to be humble enough to accept her help. God places mentors in our lives to show us how to live and to encourage us as we struggle. Titus 2:4-5 amplifies the importance of mentors: "They [older women] can train the younger women to love their husbands and children, to be self-controlled and pure, to be busy at home, to be kind, and to be subject to their husbands, so that no one will malign the word of God."

We need elasticity. Like well-kneaded dough, we need to stretch and not tear when life beats us up. When we're stretched through trials, we become windowpanes so others can see Jesus on the other side. "We are hard pressed on every side," declares the apostle Paul, "but not crushed; perplexed, but not in despair; persecuted, but not abandoned; struck down, but not destroyed. We always carry around in our body the death of Jesus, so that the life of Jesus may also be revealed in our body" (2 Corinthians 4:8-10).

Dear Lord, help me be tenacious when I fail— to keep asking for your strength when mine fails. Knead my heart until it's pliable in your hands. Open my eyes to the people you've placed in my life who point me to you, and help me to stretch and not break when trials break in like intruders. I want others to see you through the windowpane of my life.

60

PRAYING
WITHOUT CEASING

Clee

I'M ONE OF THOSE MOTHERS haunted by 1 Thessalonians 5:17 (NASB).

"Pray without ceasing," Paul urged the casserole-toting parishioners at First Thessalonica Church. In all the dictionaries I've bent pages in, ceasing means to stop. Without ceasing means to constantly be in whispered communication with Jesus—in the midst of casserole preparation, while chatting on the phone with a friend, or giving the kids a bubble bath—*any*time.

This past year I've wanted to foster a pray-without-ceasing habit. I envisioned myself looking like a cross between a quiet girl-monk and Fräulein Maria of *Sound of Music* fame—a contemplative sort who still knew how to engage life. What started as a solitary journey inside my rattled head ended as a lesson in praying for others.

Funny things happen when you try to live 1 Thessalonians 5:17. People start appearing out of the woodwork needing prayer. God crosses your path with people who are used to others saying, "Oh, that's horrible. I will pray for you." I think it delights his heart when, instead of just saying you'll pray, you actually *do* pray, right then and there.

Along this journey of spontaneous prayer, I've been forced to change my paradigms. Prayer wasn't just a thing I performed at designated prayer meetings; it became the air I breathed. Finding opportunities to pray for people became a great adventure. The following are ways God taught me how to pray for others as I attempted to "pray without ceasing."

Touch. "I don't feel good. I have a stomachache," Sophie told me. Her love language is touch, so I hugged her as I prayed. Both the words and the prayer ministered to her. When I prayed for an author friend of mine, I touched her. She said, "I'm so tired of people praying for me but never touching me. Thanks so much." Children, parents, friends—all need to feel the love of Jesus through our touch.

Today, when I placed my hand on Suzanne's shoulders—shoulders that have borne her husband's three-year joblessness—she cried. The prayer ministered to her, but it was the touch that revealed her tenderness before the Lord.

Strangers. I had almost finished my first novel. Buoyed by an endless day of frenetic typing, I couldn't stop to make dinner so I called out for pizza, much to the delight of my cheese-loving children. When the pizza man came, he looked tired, his eyes registering sadness. I tried to make light of his situation. "Too many pizzas to deliver today?" I asked. He shook his head. He told me he had a bad day peppered with family problems as he held our two pizzas.

The Lord told me to pray for him. We had a little conversation between the two of us, the Lord and I, mostly of me telling him why this was not a good idea. Finally, though, I asked the man, "Would you mind if I prayed for you?" He said no, he didn't mind, so I prayed. When I finished, he was crying. He thanked me, handed me the pizzas, and left.

A few hours later, I typed the last word of my novel and jumped up and down. (I do have some Fräulein Maria in me, after all.) In the quiet of my bed that night, the Lord whispered,

"The most eternal thing you did today wasn't finishing the novel. It was praying for the pizza man."

Cyberprayer. Today I received a very sad email from a friend. Her husband told her he did not love her and actually never did love her. I prayed for her as I responded to her via email. As I prayed, I decided to type the prayer I was praying on the spot. I've done this a lot over the past year. It's been lovely to see people being changed by simple email prayers.

I've ceased praying quite a bit this year—I wish I could decree, queenlike, that henceforth I shall pray nonstop. My frailty and my desire to be a prayer-woman intermingle daily, but I am thankful that when I do utter prayers to Jesus, he answers me by helping me touch those in need, giving me boldness to pray for strangers, and innovating my typed prayers for friends.

Dear Lord, help me to have constant communication with you throughout the day. Bring people in my life who need your touch. Stop me in the midst of the busyness so I will remember to pray for my children on the spot. Open my eyes to new and adventurous opportunities to pray—even via email.

ACKNOWLEDGMENTS

*T*HIS DEVOTIONAL REPRESENTS a long journey for me as a mother and writer. Both endeavors—mothering and writing—have been sustained by God's amazing strength. And in the midst of both, he has supplied friends and family to enable me to move forward.

In the area of mothering, I am grateful to so many. My mother gave me life. My grandmother Nana modeled hospitality. My grandmother Mary infused my life with humor. My great-grandmother, Memaw, though I never met her, taught me the joy of creativity. My great-grandmother, Mary Walker, sowed Jesus seeds in my young heart that would later blossom into an insatiable desire to serve him. I am her heritage—a follower of Jesus Christ who loves to put pen to paper.

The Lord saw fit to send me Diane Baker, my father's second wife, when I was an emerging teenager. She shared Jesus with me and modeled godly motherhood. As a young mother I met Kathy O'Neill, a woman who took me into her heart and loved me relentlessly. I don't think I'd be where I am today in terms of loving my children and knowing I am a good mother without my friend Heidi Van Dyken, who dared to tell me the truth. Her words, "Your children know you love them," have salved 11 years of mommy fear.

I often watch other mothers, hoping to glean wisdom about how I can do a better job of parenting. The woman I watch and admire the most is Renee Mills. She makes learning fun. She creates amazing birthday cakes. She builds godly character into Abigail, Caroline, and Emma Kate while her husband, Michael, attends seminary full-time and works nights. She is an amazing mother, one I hope to emulate.

The Lord has also seen fit to send me writing mentors—those people who've encouraged me and lifted my prose above mediocrity. Sandi Glahn tucked me under her writing wing. She's walked with me through this crazy journey toward publication as a friend, an editor, and a cheerleader. Chip MacGregor, to quote George Bailey, is a peach. He's prayed me through this adventure, found places for my writing, and has become my friend. Leslie Wilson, D'Ann Mateer, and Suzanne Deshchidn—all a part of our critique group, Life Sentence—have honed my writing and asked excellent questions. Leslie has been instrumental in teaching me about the business of writing; in that process we've become close friends. D'Ann has an uncanny ability to move words around and create new beginnings. Suzanne's poetry has helped me to write visually. Her editing has been invaluable.

I am thankful for the prayer warriors who have prayed for me through this book: Kevin and Renee Bailey, Gahlen and LeeAnn Crawford, Eric and Katy Gedney, Kim Griffith, Ed and Sue Harrell, Diane and Jessica Klapper, Susanne Maynes, Hud and Nancy McWilliams, Catalin and Shannon Popa, Tom and Holly Schmidt, JR and Ginger Vassar, Rod and Mary Vestal, Jodie Westfall, and Liz Wolf.

I love that Sophie crafted the "Freelance Writer" sign atop my computer. I'm honored that Aidan dedicated his first book to me. I chuckle that Julia infuses my serious life with laughter. Patrick has been a steady friend, a kindhearted encourager, and the best husband a wife could want. I'm glad we walk this marriage and parenting path together.

NOTES

1. Cowman, L.B., James Reimann, editor, *Streams in the Desert: 366 Devotional Readings* (Grand Rapids, MI: Zondervan, 1997), p. 182.

2. Allender, Dan, *How Children Raise Parents* (Colorado Springs, CO: WaterBrook Press, 2003), p. 4.

3. Frank, Don and Jan, *Unclaimed Baggage: Dealing with the Past on Your Way to a Stronger Marriage* (Colorado Springs, CO: NavPress, 2003), p. 177.

4. Chambers, Oswald, *My Utmost for His Highest* (Westwood, NJ: Barbour and Company, Inc., 1935), p. 155.

5. Lewis, C.S., *Poems* (Orlando, FL: Harcourt, Inc., 1992), p. 190.

6. Abate, Frank, editor, *The Oxford Illustrated Dictionary* (New York, NY: DK Publishing Inc., 1998), p. 957.

7. Lewis, C.S., *The Last Battle* (New York, NY: Scholastic Inc., 1956), p. 196.

8. Lewis, C.S., *Mere Christianity* (New York, NY: Macmillan Publishing Company, Inc.), p. 196.

9. Hurnard, Hannah, *Hinds' Feet on High Places* (Wheaton, IL: Tyndale House Publishers, Inc.,1993), p. 137.

10. Ibid.

11. Pipher, Mary, Ph.D., *The Shelter of Each Other: Rebuilding Our Families* (New York, NY: Ballantine Books, 1996), p. 89.

12. Frank, Leonard Roy, *Quotationary* (New York, NY: Random House, 2001), p. 791.

13. Shakespeare, William, *As You Like It* (Oxford, England: Oxford University Press, 1999), p. 27.

14. Chapman, Steven Curtis and Scotty Smith, *Speechless* (Grand Rapids, MI: Zondervan, 1999), pp. 104-05.

15. Chambers, p. 11.

16. Recer, Paul, "Baboon Mothers Do Better with Friends, Study finds," November 13, 2003, <www.msnbc.msn.com>.

17. Lawrence, Brother, *The Practice of the Presence of God* (New York, NY: Fleming H. Revell Co., 1999), p. 19.

18. Hession, Roy, *Calvary Road* (Fort Washington, PA: Christian Literature Crusade, 1950), pp. 13-14.

19. Smith, Michael, *The Secret* (Las Vegas, NV: Protea Publishing, 2002), p. 122.

20. Lewis, C.S., *The Weight of Glory and Other Addresses* (New York, NY: MacMillan, 1949), pp. 1-2.

21. Chambers, p. 49.

22. Frank, p. 243.

23. Chambers, p. 337.

24. Ibid.

25. Ibid.

26. Ibid.

27. Deere, Jack, *Surprised by the Voice of God* (Grand Rapids, MI: Zondervan Publishing House, 1996), p. 319.

28. Tada, Joni Eareckson, Stephen Estes, *When God Weeps: Why Our Sufferings Matter to the Almighty* (Grand Rapids, MI: Zondervan Publishing House, 1997), p. 108.

29. Ibid., p. 202.

30. Johnson, Samuel, *Feast of Lucy, Martyr at Syracuse* (1784), p. 304.

$\mathcal{M}$ary E. DeMuth grew up in the Pacific Northwest, where she graduated magna cum laude from Pacific Lutheran University. A former English teacher, Mary has been a stay-at-home mom and a freelance writer for more than ten years. She is also a conference speaker for Hearts at Home.

In the summer of 2004, Mary, her husband, Patrick, their three children, Sophie, Aidan, and Julia, sold their home, packed up their lives and the family cat, and moved to southern France, where they are now part of a vibrant church-planting team.

If you wish to connect mom-to-mom or woman-to-woman, Mary invites you to contact her at

maryedemuth@relevantprose.com

Other Good ———
Harvest House Reading

MAMA SAID THERE'D BE DAYS LIKE THIS
Jenn Doucette

Mothers often feel they are running as fast as they can to keep up or to stay just ahead of those who want a piece of their time, energy, and self. Author, speaker, and mother Jenn Doucette offers a humorous and insightful look at how every mom on the run can head for much–needed rest stops

THE POWER OF A PRAYING® PARENT
Stormie Omartian

Popular author Stormie Omartian offers 30 easy-to-read chapters that focus on specific areas of prayer for parents. This personal, practical guide leads the way to enriched, strong prayer lives for parents.

365 THINGS EVERY NEW MOM SHOULD KNOW
Linda Danis

This daily guide to the first year of motherhood combines prayerful, playful, and practical information to energize new moms. Features weekly devotionals and daily activities that foster a baby's physical, emotional, social, and spiritual growth.

BECOMING A SPIRIT-LED MOM
Quin Sherrer and Ruthanne Garlock

Single moms, married moms, and stepmoms—working in or outside the home—will discover God's grace, power, and strength for the daily parenting decisions they face in *Becoming a Spirit-Led Mom.*

ONE-MINUTE PRAYERS™ FOR BUSY MOMS
Designed to serve the pace and needs of everyday life, these simple prayers and inspirational verses are available when needed most. A mother's minute in prayer will free her to find refreshment in God's presence.

HARVEST HOUSE
PUBLISHERS

The Hearts at Home organization is committed to meeting the needs of women in the profession of motherhood. Founded in 1993, Hearts at Home offers a variety of resources and events to assist women in their jobs as wives and mothers.

Find out how Hearts at Home can provide you with ongoing education and encouragement in the profession of motherhood. In addition to this book, our resources include the *Hearts at Home* magazine, the *Hearts at Home* devotional, and our Hearts at Home website. Additionally, Hearts at Home events make a great getaway for individuals, moms groups, or for that special friend, sister, or sister-in-law. The regional conferences, attended by over ten thousand women each year, provide a unique, affordable, and highly encouraging weekend for the woman who takes the profession of motherhood seriously.

Hearts at Home
1509 N. Clinton Blvd.
Bloomington, Illinois 61701-1813
Phone: (309) 888-MOMS
Fax: (309) 888-4525
Email: hearts@hearts-at-home.org
Website: www.hearts-at-home.org